STIR FRY COOKBOOK

Quick and Easy Stir-fry Recipes Every Foodie Should Know

(Low Cholesterol Whole Foods Recipes Full of Antioxidants)

Jane Duffy

Published by Sharon Lohan

© **Jane Duffy**

All Rights Reserved

Stir Fry Cookbook: Quick and Easy Stir-fry Recipes Every Foodie Should Know
(Low Cholesterol Whole Foods Recipes Full of Antioxidants)

ISBN 978-1-990334-47-4

All rights reserved. No part of this guide may be reproduced in any form without permission in writing from the publisher except in the case of brief quotations embodied in critical articles or reviews.

Legal & Disclaimer

The information contained in this book is not designed to replace or take the place of any form of medicine or professional medical advice. The information in this book has been provided for educational and entertainment purposes only.

The information contained in this book has been compiled from sources deemed reliable, and it is accurate to the best of the Author's knowledge; however, the Author cannot guarantee its accuracy and validity and cannot be held liable for any errors or omissions. Changes are periodically made to this book. You must consult your doctor or get professional medical advice before using any of the suggested remedies, techniques, or information in this book.

Table of contents

Part 1 1
Introduction 2
Beef And Pepper Stir Fry With Cilantro 3
Chicken And Vegetable Stir Fry In Chili Garlic Sauce 5
Shrimp And Vegetable Stir Fry With Quail Eggs 7
Quick Noodle And Vegetable Stir Fry 9
Chicken Pepper And Bean Sprout Stir Fry On Lettuce Wrap . 11
Asian Vegetable Stir Fry 13
Quick Shrimp And Vegetable Stir-Fry 15
Beef Green Bean And Pepper Stir Fry 16
Chicken And Vegetable Stir Fry With Holy Basil 19
Chicken Liver And Pepper Stir Fry 21
Asparagus And Shrimp Stir Fry 22
Spicy Beef And Broccoli Wok Stir-Fry With Sesame 25
Spicy Bitter Gourd Stir Fry With Egg And Tomato 27
Squid And Asparagus Stir Fry With Chili 29
Shrimp And Mushroom Stir Fry In Spicy Asian Sauce 31
Garlic Chicken And Asparagus Stir Fry 33
Chicken Noodle And Veggie Stir Fry 35
Marinated Beef Tips And Veggie Stir Fry 37
Cabbage Mushroom And Pepper Stir Fry 39
Seafood Stir Fry With Water Spinach 41
Stir Fried Asparagus With Garlic 43
Spicy Shrimp And Bean Stir Fry 45

- Quick Tofu And Pepper Stir-Fry With Chili 47
- Asian-Style Seafood And Vegetable Stir-Fry 49
- Stir Fried Chicken With Black Bean And Chili Sauce 51
- Stir-Fried Beef With Green Bean And Pepper 53
- Shrimp Broccoli And Cauliflower Stir-Fry 55
- Quick Scallop And Vegetable Stir-Fry 57
- Shrimp And Vegetable Stir Fry 59
- Quick And Easy Water Spinach Stir-Fry 61
- Mixed Vegetable Stir-Fry With Chicken Liver 63
- Spicy Water Spinach Stir Fry With Cashew 65
- Beef Veggie And Udon Stir Fry 67
- Bitter Melon With Tofu And Egg Stir-Fry 69
- Stir Fried Spicy Clams With Cilantro 71
- Water Spinach And Tofu Stir-Fry With Garlic 73
- Shrimp Noodle Stir Fry With Scallion 75
- Vegetable Supreme Wok Stir-Fry 77
- Lo Mein Chicken And Vegetable Stir Fry 79
- Shrimp And Chive Wok Stir-Fry 81
- Beef Wok Stir Fry With Mixed Veggies 83
- Fresh Garden Vegetable Stir-Fry 85
- Chicken Zucchini And Eggplant Stir Fry 87
- Shrimp And Broccoli Stir-Fry Asian-Style 89
- Chow Mein Noodles With Chicken 91
- Soy Chicken And Mushroom Stir Fry 93
- Stir-Fried Vegetables With Shiitake And Tofu 95
- String Bean Stir Fry With Holy Basil 97
- Chicken Pepper And Leek Stir Fry 99

Vegetarian Noodle Stir-Fry 101

Part 2 103

Introduction 104

1. Pork Teriyaki Don 105
2. Healthy Beef Broccoli Stir Fry 107
3. Tenderloin Strips With Lemongrass 110
4. Beef Stir Fry With Long Beans & Aromatic Paste 113
5. Stir-Fried Veggie Egg Noodles With Pork 116
6. Stir-Fried Vegetables Chinese Style 118
7. Stir Fried Vermicelli With Chicken Teriyaki 120
8. Shrimp Chili Stir Fry 123
9. Chicken Rice Indian Style 125
10. Quick Stir-Fried Water Spinach With Pork Rind 127
11. Brown Rice With Stir-Fried Beef Teriyaki 129
12. Two Sauce Pork Tenders Stir Fry 131
13. Bell Pepper And Squid Stir Fry 134
14. Thai-Style Prawn Salad 136
15. Fried Rice Oriental 139
16. Beef Stir Fry With Long Beans & Aromatic Paste 141
17. Thai Squash Curry 143
18. Shrimp Lo Mein 145
19. Salmon & Snow Pea Stir Fry 147
20. Bacon Fried Rice 149

Chicken stir fry recipes 151

Stir fry chicken and vegetables 151

Kung pao chicken 153

Sweet and spicy stir fry chicken with broccoli 155

Cashew chicken stir fry with cauliflower rice 157
Simple chicken teriyaki stir fry 159
Chicken, kale and sprout stir fry 160
General Tso's chicken stir fry 162
10 minutes stir fry chicken recipe 164
Addictive Sesame Chicken 165
Adriel's Chinese Curry Chicken 167
Almond Vegetable Chicken Stir Fry 169
Anise Wine Chicken 170
Apricot Chicken Stir Fry 172
Apricot Chicken And Snow Peas 174
Asian Breakfast Stir Fry 176
Asian Carryout Noodles 178
Asian Chicken With Pasta 179
Asian Chicken With Peanuts 180
Authentic Thai Basil Chicken (Very Easy And Fast) 182
Avocado Chicken Stir Fry 183
Basil Chicken Medley 185
Bow Tie Chicken Supper 187
Broccoli Chicken Stir Fry 188
Broccoli Chicken Stir Fry For Two 190

Part 1

Introduction

Stir frying is a versatile cooking method that would often require just a few minutes of your time. The most common ingredients used are vegetables, meat, seafood, noodles, and tofu. For variety, you can mix and match some of your ingredients. You can also use herbs and spices to season your dish. Just a tip, never ever overcook your vegetables, always aim for that tender-crisp texture. This way you get to retain its freshness and also the nutrients that comes with them, since there are some vitamins and minerals are not heat stable.

Many people prefer stir frying because it is one way to cook your food healthily. You only need a small amount of oil to cook your vegetables or any other ingredients that you would want to include in your dish.

This book is a part of many cookbook series that I am writing, I hope you have fun trying out all the recipes in this book.

So now, let's get started!

Beef And Pepper Stir Fry With Cilantro

This simple yet delicious recipe with beef, pepper, and cilantro makes a great lunch or dinner. Just serve it with hot rice to complete a satisfying meal.

Preparation Time: 10 minutes
Total Time: 25 minutes
Yield: 4 servings

Ingredients
1 1/2 lbs. sirloin beef (cut into thin strips)
2 Tbsp. dark soy sauce
1/4 tsp. freshly ground black pepper
2 Tbsp. peanut oil
1 medium onion (thinly sliced)
2 cloves garlic (minced)
1 medium red bell pepper
1 medium green bell pepper

1 medium yellow pepper
1/4 cup cilantro (chopped)
1/4 cup oyster sauce
salt and freshly ground black pepper to taste

Method
1. Combine the beef and soy sauce in a medium bowl. Mix well. Season with pepper.
2. Heat peanut oil in a large skillet or wok over medium heat. Stir-fry the onion and garlic for 1-2 minutes.
3. Add the beef strips and cook for 5 minutes, stirring often.
4. Add the bell peppers, cilantro, and oyster sauce. Cook, stirring occasionally for about 7-10 minutes. Remove from heat. Season with salt and pepper, to taste.
5. Transfer to a serving dish.
6. Serve and enjoy.

Chicken And Vegetable Stir Fry In Chili Garlic Sauce

This stir-fried chicken and vegetable with chili garlic sauce makes a wonderful dinner in minutes.

Preparation Time: 10 minutes
Total Time: 25 minutes
Yield: 8 servings

Ingredients
2 Tbsp. olive oil
1 large white onion (sliced)
1 tsp. garlic (minced)
1 tsp. chili flakes
1/2 tsp. cumin (ground)
2 lbs. chicken breast fillet (cut into strips)
1 medium zucchini (thinly sliced)
1 medium red bell pepper (deseeded and cut into 1-inch pieces)

1 medium green bell pepper (deseeded and cut into 1-inch pieces)
2 Tbsp. butter
1/4 cup tomato paste
1/4 cup ketchup
salt and freshly ground black pepper

Method
1. In a wok, heat vegetable oil over medium-high heat. Stir-fry white onion and garlic for 3 minutes. Add the chili flakes and cumin. Cook, stirring for another 1 minute.
2. Add the chicken breast. Cook, stirring often for about 7 minutes.
3. Add the zucchini and bell peppers. Cook for 7 minutes, stirring occasionally.
4. Stir in butter, tomato paste, and ketchup. Season with salt and pepper to taste. Cook further 5 minutes.
5. Transfer to a serving dish.
6. Serve and enjoy.

Shrimp And Vegetable Stir Fry With Quail Eggs

This delightful seafood and vegetable recipe with quail eggs makes a great lunch or dinner.

Preparation Time: 10 minutes
Total Time: 25 minutes
Yield: 6 servings

Ingredients
2 Tbsp. vegetable oil
1 lb. shrimps (peeled and deveined)
2 shallots (sliced)
2 cloves garlic (minced)
1/2 tsp. fresh ginger root (grated)
1 medium carrot (cut into thin flowerets)
4 oz. snap peas (trimmed)
2 cups broccoli (cut into florets)
1 cup button mushrooms (halved)
12 quail eggs (boiled and peeled)
salt and freshly ground black pepper

Method
1. Heat oil in a wok or large skillet over medium-high heat. Stir-fry the shrimps for 2-3 minutes. Remove using a slotted spoon into a clean plate. Set aside.
2. Using the same wok or skillet, stir fry shallots, garlic, and ginger for 3-5 minutes over medium-high heat.
3. Add the carrot, snap peas, broccoli, and button mushrooms. Cook for 7 minutes, stirring occasionally.
4. Add the quail eggs and cooked shrimps. Cook for another 3 minutes. Season with salt and pepper to taste. Remove from heat.
5. Serve and enjoy.

Quick Noodle And Vegetable Stir Fry

This noodle dish is very popular in Asia, it's very easy to prepare and filling.

Preparation Time: 10 minutes
Total Time: 25 minutes
Yield: 6 servings

Ingredients
2 Tbsp. vegetable oil
1 medium red onion (chopped)
1 tsp. garlic (minced)
1 tsp. fresh ginger (grated)
2 cups broccoli florets
1 cup green beans (trimmed and cut into 1-inch pieces)
1 medium carrot (cut into thin strips)
1 stalk celery (diced)
2 cups vegetable stock or chicken stock (reduced-sodium)
1 cup water

2 Tbsp. light soy sauce
1 Tbsp. oyster sauce
10 oz. egg noodles (dry)
1/4 cup scallions (chopped)
freshly ground black pepper

Method
1. Heat vegetable oil in a wok over medium-high heat. Stir-fry onion, garlic, and ginger for 5 minutes.
2. Add the broccoli, green beans, carrot, and celery. Cook, stirring for 2-3 minutes.
3. Add chicken stock, water, soy sauce, and oyster sauce. Bring to a boil over high heat.
4. Add the egg noodles and cook, stirring occasionally until almost tender.
5. Add the scallions. Cook further 3 minutes, stirring often. Season with pepper to taste. Remove from heat.
6. Transfer to a serving dish.
7. Serve and enjoy.

Chicken Pepper And Bean Sprout Stir Fry On Lettuce Wrap

This stir fry recipe made with chicken, pepper, and bean sprouts is perfect for your lunchbox. It's delicious and nutritious as well.

Preparation Time: 10 minutes
Total Time: 30 minutes
Yield: 4-6 servings

Ingredients
2 Tbsp. peanut oil
2 shallots (chopped)
1 tsp. garlic (minced)
1 lb. chicken breast fillet (cut into thin strips)
1 medium green bell pepper (deseeded and cut into strips)
2 Tbsp. Tamari or regular soy sauce
2 Tbsp. rice wine vinegar
2 cups mungbean sprouts

1 head iceberg lettuce (leaves separated)
salt and freshly ground black pepper to taste

Method
1. In a wok or large skillet, heat peanut oil over medium-high heat. Stir-fry shallots and garlic for 3 minutes or until fragrant.
2. Add the chicken strips and cook for 7 minutes or until browned, stirring frequently.
3. Add the bell pepper, Tamari, and rice wine vinegar. Cook for 5 minutes, stirring occasionally.
4. Add the mungbean sprouts. Cook further 3-5 minutes. Season with salt and pepper, to taste.
5. Place 2 tablespoons of stir-fried chicken and vegetable mixture onto each lettuce leaf until everything has been used up.
6. Serve in a serving dish and enjoy.

Asian Vegetable Stir Fry

This appetizing stir-fry recipe with mixed vegetables is packed with flavor and nutrition!

Preparation Time: 15 minutes
Total Time: 25 minutes
Yield: 3-4 servings

Ingredients
2 Tbsp. vegetable oil
1 tsp. garlic (minced)
2 medium carrots (cut into thin strips)
2 cups button mushrooms (sliced)
2 leeks (thinly sliced)
4 cups water spinach (torn into 3-inch pieces)
1 head Chinese cabbage (cut diagonally)
2 Tbsp. oyster sauce
1 tsp. sesame oil
salt and freshly ground black pepper

Method
1. In a wok or large skillet, heat vegetable oil over medium-high heat. Stir-fry garlic for 3 minutes.
2. Add the carrots, mushrooms, and leeks. Cook for about 7 minutes, stirring frequently.
3. Add the water spinach, Chinese cabbage, and oyster sauce. Cook, stirring for 3-5 minutes.
4. Stir in sesame oil. Remove from heat. Season with salt and pepper, to taste.
5. Transfer to a serving dish.
6. Serve and enjoy.

Quick Shrimp And Vegetable Stir-Fry

This Asian-inspired stir-fry recipe is so good and very easy to cook. Perfect dish for busy weeknights!

Preparation Time: 10 minutes
Total Time: 20 minutes
Yield: 4 servings

Ingredients
3 Tbsp. vegetable oil (divided)
1 medium white onion (chopped)
3 cloves garlic (minced)
1 lb. fresh shrimps (peeled and deveined)
2 medium carrots (cut into thin strips)
4 oz. snap peas (trimmed)
salt and freshly ground black pepper

Method

1. In a wok, heat 1 tablespoon vegetable oil over medium-high heat. Stir-fry the shrimps for 2-3 minutes. Transfer to a clean plate and set aside.
2. Heat remaining oil in the same wok. Cook the onion and garlic for 3 minutes, stirring frequently.
3. Add the carrot and snap peas. Cook, stirring for 5-7 minutes.
4. Return the shrimps into the wok and cook for another 2-3 minutes. Remove from heat. Season with salt and pepper to taste.
5. Transfer to a serving platter.
6. Serve and enjoy.

Beef Green Bean And Pepper Stir Fry

This wonderful stir-fry with beef, green beans, and pepper has a nice blend of flavors.

Preparation Time: 10 minutes
Total Time: 25 minutes
Yield: 4 servings

Ingredients
1 1/2 lbs. sirloin beef (cut into thin strips)
2 Tbsp. light soy sauce
1 tsp. Worcestershire sauce
1/4 tsp. freshly ground black pepper
2 Tbsp. olive oil
1 large white onion (thinly sliced)
2-3 cloves garlic (minced)
1 medium red bell pepper (thinly sliced)
1 medium carrot (thinly sliced)
4 oz. green beans (cut diagonally)
1 cup button mushrooms (quartered)
1/4 cup oyster sauce
salt and freshly ground black pepper to taste
toasted sesame seeds

Method
1. Place the beef in a medium bowl. Add soy sauce and Worcestershire sauce. Mix well. Season with pepper.
2. Heat olive oil in a large skillet or wok over medium heat. Stir-fry the onion and garlic for 3 minutes.
3. Add the beef strips and cook for 7 minutes, stirring often.
4. Add the red bell pepper, carrot, green beans, mushrooms, and oyster sauce. Cook, stirring occasionally for about 7-10 minutes. Remove from heat. Season with salt and pepper, to taste.

5. Transfer to a serving dish. Sprinkle with toasted sesame seeds.
6. Serve and enjoy.

Chicken And Vegetable Stir Fry With Holy Basil

This simple yet flavorful dish with chicken and veggies is truly satisfying!

Preparation Time: 10 minutes
Total Time: 25 minutes
Yield: 8 servings

Ingredients
2 Tbsp. vegetable oil
1 medium onion (thinly sliced)
2 cloves garlic (minced)
2 lbs. chicken breast fillet (cut into thin strips)
1 medium red bell pepper (thinly sliced)
1 medium yellow pepper (thinly sliced)
2 leeks (thinly sliced)
2 medium carrot (thinly sliced)
2 stalks celery (diced)
2 cups mungbean sprouts
1/2 cup holy basil (leaves separated)

2 Tbsp. dark soy sauce
2 Tbsp. rice wine vinegar
1/4 cup dry roasted cashew nuts (coarsely chopped)
salt and freshly ground black pepper to taste

Method
1. Heat vegetable oil in a large skillet or wok over medium heat. Stir-fry the onion and garlic for 3 minutes.
2. Add the chicken strips. Cook for 7 minutes, stirring often.
3. Add the bell peppers, leeks, carrots, and celery. Cook for 5-7 minutes.
4. Add the mungbean sprouts and holy basil leaves. Cook further 3 minutes, stirring often. Season with salt and pepper, to taste.
5. Transfer to a serving dish. Sprinkle with chopped cashew nuts.
6. Serve and enjoy.

Chicken Liver And Pepper Stir Fry

Quick, tasty, and easy stir-fry recipe has a unique taste that you will surely love!

Preparation Time: 10 minutes
Total Time: 25 minutes
Yield: 4 servings

Ingredients
1 1/2 lbs. chicken (cut into small pieces)
2 Tbsp. dark soy sauce
1/4 cup fresh lemon juice
1/4 tsp. freshly ground black pepper
2 Tbsp. olive oil
1 large red onion (sliced)
2 cloves garlic (minced)
1 medium yellow pepper (deseeded and sliced)
1 medium red bell pepper (deseeded and sliced)
1 Tbsp. Worcestershire sauce
salt and freshly ground black pepper

Method
1. Combine the chicken liver, soy sauce, and lemon juice in a medium bowl. Mix well. Season with pepper.
2. Heat vegetable oil in a large skillet or wok over medium heat. Stir-fry the red onion and garlic for 3 minutes.
3. Add the chicken liver and cook for 7-8 minutes, stirring often.
4. Add the bell peppers and Worcestershire sauce. Cook, stirring occasionally for another 7-8 minutes. Remove from heat. Season with salt and pepper, to taste.
5. Transfer to a serving dish.
6. Serve and enjoy.

Asparagus And Shrimp Stir Fry

This recipe is so simple and only needs a few simple *ingredients* yet it still yields an awesome dish!

Preparation Time: 10 minutes
Total Time: 20 minutes
Yield: 4-5 servings

Ingredients
3 Tbsp. olive oil
2 shallots (chopped)
1 tsp. garlic (minced)
1 medium tomato (chopped)
1/2 tsp. fresh ginger root (grated)
1 lb. fresh shrimp (peeled and deveined)
1 lb. asparagus (trimmed and cut into 2-inch pieces)
1/2 cup vegetable stock (unsalted)
salt and freshly ground black pepper

Method
1. Heat 1 tablespoon vegetable oil in a large skillet or wok over medium heat. Cook the shrimps for 2-3 minutes. Transfer to a clean plate and set aside.
2. In the same skillet or wok, heat remaining oil. Stir-fry the shallots and garlic for 1-2 minutes.
3. Add the tomato and ginger. Cook, stirring for 3 minutes.
4. Add the asparagus and vegetable stock. Cook for 7-10 minutes or until crisp-tender, stirring occasionally.

5. Add the cooked shrimps and cook for another 2-3 minutes. Season with salt and pepper, to taste. Remove from heat.
6. Transfer to a serving dish.
7. Serve and enjoy.

Spicy Beef And Broccoli Wok Stir-Fry With Sesame

This Asian-inspired beef and broccoli stir-fry recipe has a mild kick to it that you will surely enjoy.

Preparation Time: 10 minutes
Total Time: 25 minutes
Yield: 4 servings

Ingredients
2 Tbsp. vegetable oil (divided)
1 lb. sirloin beef (thinly sliced)
1 medium onion (thinly sliced)
1 tsp. garlic (minced)
1 head broccoli (cut into small florets)
1/2 cup beef stock (unsalted)
2 Tbsp. soy sauce
1 Tbsp. chili garlic paste
1 tsp. sesame oil
salt and freshly ground black pepper

toasted sesame seeds

Method

1. Heat 1 tablespoon oil in a wok over medium-high heat. Cook the beef for 7 to 10 minutes or until browned, stirring often. Transfer to a plate and cover to keep warm.
2. Heat remaining vegetable oil in the same wok. Stir-fry onion and garlic for 3 minutes.
3. Add the broccoli, beef stock, soy sauce, and chili garlic paste. Cook, stirring occasionally for 8 to 10 minutes or until broccoli is crisp-tender.
4. Add the beef and cook for another 2 to 3 minutes. Season with salt and pepper to taste. Stir in sesame oil. Remove from heat.
5. Transfer to a serving dish. Sprinkle with sesame seeds.
6. Serve and enjoy.

Spicy Bitter Gourd Stir Fry With Egg And Tomato

Bitter gourd or bitter melon is packed with nutrients that offers many health benefits. This stir-fry recipe made with eggs, onion, and tomatoes is a must try!

Preparation Time: 10 minutes
Total Time: 30 minutes
Yield: 4 servings

Ingredients
2 Tbsp. vegetable oil (divided)
2 medium bitter gourd
1 medium onion (thinly sliced)
1 tsp. garlic (minced)
2 medium tomatoes (chopped)
2 medium eggs (beaten)
salt and freshly ground black pepper

Method
1. Cut the bitter gourds lengthwise. Scoop out and throw away the white part with the seeds using a spoon. Slice thinly crosswise.
2. Heat vegetable oil in a non-stick fry pan or skillet over medium-high heat. Stir-fry onion, garlic, and tomatoes for 5 minutes.
3. Add the sliced bitter gourd. Cook for about 7 to 10 minutes, stirring occasionally.
4. Stir in beaten egg. Cook further 3 minutes. Season with salt and pepper to taste.
5. Transfer in a serving platter.
6. Serve and enjoy.

Squid And Asparagus Stir Fry With Chili

This seafood stir-fry recipe is absolutely delicious!

Preparation Time: 15 minutes
Total Time: 25 minutes
Yield: 8 servings

Ingredients
2 Tbsp. vegetable oil (divided)
2 shallots (chopped)
1 tsp. garlic (minced)
1 tsp. fresh ginger root (grated)
2 lbs. squid (cleaned and cut into rings)
1 lb. asparagus (trimmed and cut into 1-inch pieces)
2 Tbsp. soy sauce
2 Tbsp. rice wine vinegar
2 tsp. Worcestershire sauce
1 red hot chili pepper (thinly sliced)
1/4 cup cilantro (coarsely chopped)
salt and freshly ground black pepper

Method
1. Heat 1 tablespoon vegetable oil in a wok or large skillet over medium-high heat. Stir-fry shallots, garlic, and ginger for 3 minutes.
2. Add the squid, soy sauce, rice wine vinegar, Worcestershire sauce, and chili. Cook, stirring for 3 to 5 minutes. Transfer to a clean plate.
3. In the same skillet, heat remaining oil over medium-high heat. Cook the asparagus and cilantro for 8 to 10 minutes or until the asparagus is crisp-tender, stirring frequently.
4. Return the squid into the skillet and cook for another 2 to 3 minutes. Season with salt and pepper to taste. Remove from heat.
5. Transfer to a serving dish.
6. Serve and enjoy.

Shrimp And Mushroom Stir Fry In Spicy Asian Sauce

This wonderful seafood recipe makes a great appetizer or main.

Preparation Time: 10 minutes
Total Time: 20 minutes
Yield: 4 servings

Ingredients
2 Tbsp. butter
1 medium onion (thinly sliced)
2 cloves garlic (thinly sliced)
1 lb. shrimps (peeled, deveined, and tails intact)
1 cup button mushrooms (halved)
1/4 cup ketchup
2 Tbsp. oyster sauce
1 tsp. brown sugar
1 Tbsp. chili garlic paste
1 cup green onions (cut into 2-inch pieces)

salt and freshly ground black pepper

Method
1. Melt butter in a wok or skillet over medium heat. Stir-fry onion and garlic for 3 minutes.
2. Add the shrimps, ketchup, oyster sauce, brown sugar, chili paste, and green onions. Cook for 5 minutes, stirring often. Season with salt and pepper to taste. Remove from heat.
3. Transfer to a serving dish.
4. Serve and enjoy.

Garlic Chicken And Asparagus Stir Fry

This awesome chicken and asparagus dish is perfect for quick dinners.

Preparation Time: 10 minutes
Total Time: 25 minutes
Yield: 4 servings

Ingredients
2 Tbsp. olive oil
2 Tbsp. garlic (chopped)
1 lb. chicken breast fillet (cut into strips)
1 lb. asparagus (trimmed and cut into 1-1/2 inch pieces)
2 Tbsp. light soy sauce
2 tsp. Worcestershire sauce
1/2 tsp. garlic powder
1/2 tsp. ginger powder
salt and freshly ground black pepper
toasted garlic (for topping)

Method

1. Heat olive oil in a wok or skillet over medium heat. Stir-fry garlic for 3 minutes or until toasted and golden brown. Transfer to a small plate or bowl. Set aside.
2. In the same wok, cook chicken over medium-high heat for 5 to 7 minutes, stirring often.
3. Add the asparagus, soy sauce, Worcestershire sauce, ginger powder, and garlic powder. Cook further 8 to 10 minutes, stirring occasionally. Season with salt and pepper to taste. Remove from heat.
4. Transfer to a serving platter. Sprinkle with reserved toasted garlic.
5. Serve and enjoy.

Chicken Noodle And Veggie Stir Fry

This stir fried noodle dish with chicken and vegetables is perfect for any occasion!

Preparation Time: 10 minutes
Total Time: 30 minutes
Yield: 4-6 servings

Ingredients
2 Tbsp. vegetable oil
2 shallots (sliced)
1 tsp. garlic (minced)
12 oz. chicken breast (cut into thin strips)
1 medium carrot (cut into thin strips)
1 celery stalk (diced)
1 cup chicken stock
1 cup water
2 Tbsp. oyster sauce
10 oz. egg noodles
1 handful mungbean sprouts
1 handful snap peas (trimmed)

1/4 cup cilantro (chopped)
freshly ground black pepper

Method
1. Heat oil in a wok over medium-high heat. Stir-fry shallots and garlic for 3 minutes.
2. Add chicken and cook for about 5 to 7 minutes.
3. Add carrot and celery. Cook, stirring for 3 minutes.
4. Add chicken stock, water, and oyster sauce. Bring to a boil.
5. Add the egg noodles and cook until almost tender.
6. Add the mungbean sprouts, snap peas, and cilantro. Cook further 3 to 5 minutes, stirring often. Season with salt and pepper to taste. Remove from heat.
7. Transfer to a serving dish.
8. Serve and enjoy.

Marinated Beef Tips And Veggie Stir Fry

This stir-fried beef with mixed vegetables is a must try!

Preparation Time: 10 minutes
Total Time: 25 minutes
Yield: 6 servings

Ingredients
1 lb. beef sirloin (cut into thin strips)
2 Tbsp. Tamari or regular soy sauce
2 Tbsp. rice wine vinegar
2 tsp. brown sugar
1/4 tsp. freshly ground black pepper
2 Tbsp. peanut oil (divided)
1 medium onion (chopped)
3 large cloves garlic (minced)
1 medium carrot (thinly sliced)
8 oz. green beans (trimmed, cut diagonally to 1 ½-inch pieces)
1 small head broccoli (cut into small florets)
1/2 cup beef stock

2 Tbsp. oyster sauce
salt and freshly ground black pepper

Method
1. Combine beef, Tamari, rice wine vinegar, brown sugar, and pepper in a non-reactive bowl. Cover and refrigerate for at least an hour.
2. Heat 1 tablespoon oil in a wok over medium-high heat. Cook the beef strips until browned, about 7 minutes. Transfer to a plate and set aside.
3. In the same wok, heat remaining oil and stir-fry onion and garlic for 3 minutes.
4. Add the carrots, green beans, broccoli, beef stock, and oyster sauce. Cook, stirring occasionally for 10 minutes or until vegetables are crisp-tender.
5. Return the beef and cook further 3 minutes. Season with salt and pepper to taste.
6. Transfer to a plate.
7. Serve immediately and enjoy.

Cabbage Mushroom And Pepper Stir Fry

This vegetable dish makes a perfect side dish to grilled meat, fish, or poultry!

Preparation Time: 10 minutes
Total Time: 25 minutes
Yield: 4 servings

Ingredients
2 Tbsp. olive oil
1 medium red onion (chopped)
3 large cloves garlic (minced)
2 medium tomatoes (chopped)
1 medium red bell pepper (deseeded and thinly sliced)
1 cup button mushrooms (thinly sliced)
1 head cabbage (shredded)
1/2 cup chicken stock
salt and freshly ground black pepper

Method

1. Heat olive oil in a wok over medium-high heat. Stir-fry onion, garlic, and tomatoes for 5 minutes.
2. Add the bell pepper, mushrooms, cabbage, and chicken stock. Cook, stirring occasionally for about 8 to 10 minutes or until vegetables are crisp-tender. Season with salt and pepper to taste. Remove from heat.
3. Transfer to a serving dish.
4. Serve immediately and enjoy.

Seafood Stir Fry With Water Spinach

This seafood stir-fry recipe with water spinach is so delicious and nutritious!

Preparation Time: 10 minutes
Total Time: 20 minutes
Yield: 8 servings

Ingredients
2 Tbsp. vegetable oil (divided)
2 shallots (chopped)
1 tsp. garlic (minced)
1 tsp. fresh ginger root (grated)
2 medium tomatoes (chopped)
1 lb. fresh squid (cleaned and cut into rings)
1 lb. fresh shrimps (peeled and deveined)
1 lb. water spinach (trimmed and cut into 1-inch pieces)
2 Tbsp. soy sauce

2 Tbsp. white vinegar
2 tsp. Worcestershire sauce
1/4 cup scallions (chopped)
salt and freshly ground black pepper

Method
1. Heat vegetable oil in a wok or large skillet over medium-high heat. Stir-fry shallots, garlic, ginger, and tomatoes for 5 minutes.
2. Add the squid, shrimps, soy sauce, white vinegar, and Worcestershire sauce. Cook, stirring for 2 to 3 minutes.
3. Add the water spinach and scallions. Cook, stirring for another 3 to 5 minutes. Transfer to a serving dish.
4. Serve and enjoy.

Stir Fried Asparagus With Garlic

This is a yummy beginner-friendly stir-fry recipe that calls for only a few *ingredients*.

Preparation Time: 10 minutes
Total Time: 20 minutes
Yield: 3-4 servings

Ingredients
2 Tbsp. olive oil
1 medium red onion (chopped)
3 Tbsp. garlic (chopped)
1 lb. asparagus (trimmed and cut into 1-1/2 inch pieces)
2 Tbsp. oyster sauce
salt and freshly ground black pepper

Method

1. Heat olive oil in a wok or large skillet over medium heat. Stir-fry onion and garlic for 3 minutes.
2. Add the asparagus and oyster sauce. Cook, stirring from time to time, for about 8 to 10 minutes. Season with salt and pepper, to taste. Remove from heat.
3. Transfer to a serving platter.
4. Serve and enjoy.

Spicy Shrimp And Bean Stir Fry

This spicy seafood and vegetable stir-fry recipe is definitely a must try!

Preparation Time: 10 minutes
Total Time: 20 minutes
Yield: 4 servings

Ingredients
2 Tbsp. vegetable oil (divided)
1 lb. fresh shrimps (peeled and deveined)
2 shallots (chopped)
1 tsp. garlic (minced)
1 lb. green beans (trimmed and cut diagonally into 1-inch pieces)
1 cup mungbean sprouts
2 Tbsp. soy sauce
2 red hot chili peppers (thinly sliced)
salt and freshly ground black pepper

Method

1. Heat 1 tablespoon vegetable oil in a wok or large skillet over medium-high heat. Cook the shrimps for 2 to 3 minutes. Transfer to a clean plate.
2. In the same wok, heat remaining oil over medium-high heat. Stir-fry shallots and garlic for 3 minutes.
3. Add the green beans and mungbean sprouts. Cook for 5 minutes.
4. Return the shrimps into the wok and add the chili peppers. Cook further 2 to 3 minutes, stirring often. Season with salt and pepper to taste. Remove from heat.
5. Transfer to a serving dish.
6. Serve and enjoy.

Quick Tofu And Pepper Stir-Fry With Chili

This delightful stir-fry recipe with tofu makes an awesome appetizer or main.

Preparation Time: 10 minutes
Total Time: 20 minutes
Yield: 4-6 servings

Ingredients
4 Tbsp. canola oil (divided)
1 (16 oz.) package firm tofu (cut into 1-inch cubes)
1 medium red onion (chopped)
1 tsp. garlic (crushed)
1 medium green bell pepper (deseeded and thinly sliced)
1 medium red bell pepper (deseeded and thinly sliced)
2 Tbsp. soy sauce
1 red hot chili pepper (thinly sliced)
1/2 cup fresh chili leaves (torn)
salt and freshly ground black pepper

Method
1. Heat 2 tablespoons oil in a large non-stick fry pan over medium-high heat. Cook tofu until it becomes golden brown. Transfer to a clean plate.
2. Using the same pan, heat remaining oil. Stir-fry onion and garlic.
3. Add the bell peppers, tofu, soy sauce, chili pepper, and chili leaves. Cook for another 5 to 7 minutes, stirring often. Season with salt and pepper to taste.
4. Transfer to a serving dish.
5. Serve and enjoy.

Asian-Style Seafood And Vegetable Stir-Fry

A great tasting seafood and vegetable dish that is good for lunch or dinner!

Preparation Time: 10 minutes
Total Time: 25 minutes
Yield: 8 servings

Ingredients
1 lb. fresh shrimp (peeled, deveined, and tails intact)
1 lb. fresh squid (cleaned)
3 Tbsp. peanut oil (divided)
2 shallots (chopped)
1 tsp. garlic (minced)
1 medium carrot (cut into flowerets)
1 lb. asparagus (trimmed and cut into small pieces)
1/2 cup chicken stock
1 tsp. sesame oil
salt and freshly ground black pepper

Method
1. Remove and discard skin from the squid then slice it in half. Score the insides to make a crisscross pattern, then cut into small pieces. Cut the squid tentacles into small pieces.
2. Heat 1 Tbsp. peanut oil in a wok over medium-high heat.
3. Add the shrimp and squid. Stir-fry for 1-2 minutes. Transfer to a clean plate.
4. Heat the remaining oil in the same wok, stir-fry shallots and garlic for 3 minutes.
5. Add the carrot and asparagus. Cook, stirring often for 5 to 7 minutes or until they are crisp-tender.
6. Return the seafood to the wok, add the chicken stock. Cook for another 2 to 3 minutes or until the seafood is heated through. Season with salt and pepper to taste. Stir in sesame oil. Remove from heat.
7. Transfer to a serving dish.
8. Serve and enjoy.

Stir Fried Chicken With Black Bean And Chili Sauce

This quick chicken stir-fry makes a fantastic rice topping!

Preparation Time: 10 minutes
Total Time: 20 minutes
Yield: 4 servings

Ingredients
2 Tbsp. peanut oil
1 medium white onion (chopped)
2 cloves garlic
1 lb. chicken breast fillet (cut into strips)
1/4 cup canned black beans
2 Tbsp. soy sauce
2 Tbsp. sweet chili sauce
1/2 tsp. ginger powder
2 Tbsp. cilantro (chopped)
2 Tbsp. toasted sesame seeds

salt and freshly ground black pepper

Method
1. Heat peanut oil in a wok or skillet over medium heat. Stir-fry onion and garlic for 3 minutes.
2. Add the chicken, black beans, soy sauce, sweet chili sauce, and ginger powder. Cook for 10 minutes, stirring often.
3. Add cilantro and cook for another 2 to 3 minutes. Season with salt and pepper to taste. Remove from heat.
4. Transfer to a serving dish. Sprinkle with toasted sesame seeds.
5. Serve and enjoy.

Stir-Fried Beef With Green Bean And Pepper

This stir-fry recipe is perfect for potlucks, everyone will surely love it!

Preparation Time: 10 minutes
Total Time: 25 minutes
Yield: 4 servings

Ingredients
1 lb. beef sirloin (cut into thin strips)
2 Tbsp. reduced-sodium soy sauce
2 Tbsp. lemon juice
1 Tbsp. brown sugar
1/4 tsp. freshly ground black pepper
2 Tbsp. vegetable oil (divided)
1 medium onion (chopped)
3 large cloves garlic (minced)
2 medium yellow bell pepper (deseeded and thinly sliced)
8 oz. green beans (trimmed, cut diagonally to 1 ½-inch pieces)
2 leeks (thinly sliced diagonally)

1/2 cup beef stock
2 Tbsp. oyster sauce
salt and freshly ground black pepper

Method
1. Combine the beef, soy sauce, lemon juice, brown sugar, and pepper in a medium bowl.
2. Heat 1 tablespoon oil in a large skillet over medium-high heat. Stir-fry beef until they are brown, about 7 to 8 minutes.
3. In the same skillet, heat remaining oil and stir-fry onion and garlic for 3 minutes.
4. Add the bell peppers and green beans. Cook, stirring for 5 minutes.
5. Return the beef into the skillet and add the leeks. Cook further 3 minutes. Season with salt and pepper to taste. Remove from heat.
6. Transfer to a serving dish.
7. Serve and enjoy.

Shrimp Broccoli And Cauliflower Stir-Fry

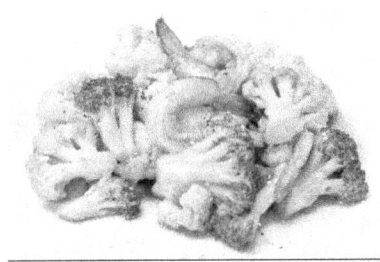

This tasty and healthy seafood dish with veggies is can be served with some noodles or as a rice topping!

Preparation Time: 10 minutes
Total Time: 25 minutes
Yield: 8 servings

Ingredients
2 Tbsp. peanut oil
1 shallots onion (chopped)
3 cloves garlic (minced)
1 lb. fresh shrimps (peeled, deveined, and tails intact)
1 head cauliflower (cut into small florets)
1 head broccoli florets (cut into small florets)
2/3 cup chicken stock
2 Tbsp. Kekap Manis (Indonesian sweet soy sauce)
1 tsp. sesame oil
salt and freshly ground black pepper

toasted sesame seeds

Method
1. Heat 1 tablespoon oil in a wok over medium-high heat. Cook the shrimps for 3 minutes. Transfer to a clean plate.
2. Using the same wok, heat remaining oil and stir-fry shallots and garlic for 3 to 4 minutes.
3. Add the broccoli, cauliflower, and Kekap Manis. Cook for 8 to 10 minutes or until crisp-tender, stirring frequently.
4. Return the shrimps into the wok and cook further 2 to 3 minutes. Stir in sesame oil. Season with salt and pepper to taste. Remove from heat.
5. Transfer to a serving platter. Sprinkle with toasted sesame seeds.
6. Serve and enjoy.

Quick Scallop And Vegetable Stir-Fry

This wonderful dish with scallops and vegetables makes an awesome rice topping or serve with noodles to complete the meal.

Preparation Time: 10 minutes
Total Time: 20 minutes
Yield: 4 servings

Ingredients
2 Tbsp. vegetable oil
1 lb. dry scallops
1 medium white onion (chopped)
3 cloves garlic (minced)
1 medium tomato (diced)
1 cup asparagus tips (trimmed and cut into small pieces)
1 cup baby corn (cut into 1-inch pieces)
1 medium red bell pepper (diced)
1/4 cup dry white wine

2 Tbsp. reduced-sodium soy sauce
1/4 cup cilantro (coarsely chopped)
salt and freshly ground black pepper

Method
1. Heat 1 tablespoon vegetable oil in a large non-stick pan or skillet over medium-high heat. Sear the scallops for a few minutes or until opaque and slightly toasted. Transfer to a clean plate.
2. Heat remaining oil in the same skillet. Stir-fry the onion, garlic, and tomato for 5 minutes.
3. Add the asparagus tips, baby corn, red bell pepper, white wine, soy sauce, and cilantro. Cook, for about 7 to 8 minutes, stirring occasionally.
4. Return the scallops into the skillet and cook further 2 to 3 minutes. Season with salt and pepper, to taste.
5. Transfer in a serving dish.
6. Serve and enjoy.

Shrimp And Vegetable Stir Fry

Shrimp stir-fry with veggies made fresh, fast, and delicious!

Preparation Time: 15 minutes
Total Time: 20 minutes
Yield: 4 servings

Ingredients
2 Tbsp. peanut oil
1 lb. fresh shrimps (peeled and deveined)
4 oz. snap peas or snow peas (trimmed)
2 cups mungbean sprouts
1/2 cup onion (chopped)
1 tsp. garlic (minced)
1 Tbsp. Worcestershire sauce
1/2 tsp. ginger powder
salt and freshly ground black pepper

Method
1. Heat 1 tablespoon peanut oil in a wok or skillet over medium-high heat. Stir-fry shrimps for 2 to 3 minutes. Transfer to a clean plate. Set aside.
2. In the same wok, heat remaining oil. Stir-fry onion and garlic for 3 minutes.
3. Add the snap peas, mungbean sprouts, Worcestershire sauce, and ginger powder. Cook, stirring often for 5 minutes.
4. Return the shrimps and cook for another 2 minutes. Season with salt and pepper to taste. Remove from heat.
5. Transfer to a serving platter.
6. Serve and enjoy.

Quick And Easy Water Spinach Stir-Fry

This scrumptious vegetable stir-fry recipe with water spinach makes a perfect side to your steamed fish.

Preparation Time: 10 minutes
Total Time: 20 minutes
Yield: 6 servings

Ingredients
2 Tbsp. olive oil
1 medium red onion (chopped)
2 Tbsp. garlic (chopped)
2 lbs. water spinach (cut into 3-inch pieces, large stems removed)
1/4 cup soy sauce
1/4 cup white vinegar
2 tsp. brown sugar
salt and freshly ground black pepper

Method

1. Heat oil in a wok over medium-high heat. Stir-fry onion and garlic for 3 minutes.
2. Add the soy sauce, vinegar, and brown sugar. Mix well.
3. Add the water spinach and cook for 5 minutes, stirring occasionally. Season with salt and pepper to taste. Remove from heat.
4. Transfer to a serving dish.
5. Serve and enjoy.

Mixed Vegetable Stir-Fry With Chicken Liver

This is a wonderful dish that combines the flavor of different vegetables and chicken liver.

Preparation Time: 10 minutes
Total Time: 25 minutes
Yield: 6-8 servings

Ingredients
2 Tbsp. vegetable oil
2 shallots (sliced)
1 tsp. garlic (minced)
12 oz. chicken liver (cut into small pieces)
4 oz. snap peas (trimmed)
1 cup button mushrooms (sliced)
1 cup baby corn (cut into small pieces)
1 medium carrot (cut into flowerets)
1 medium red bell pepper (cut into 1-inch pieces)
1/2 head broccoli (cut into small florets)
1/2 head cauliflower (cut into small florets)
1/2 head cabbage (shredded)

3 Tbsp. oyster sauce
1 1/2 tsp. sesame oil
salt and freshly ground black pepper

Method
1. Heat vegetable oil in a wok over medium-high heat. Stir-fry shallots and garlic for 3 minutes.
2. Add the chicken liver and cook for 5 minutes, stirring often.
3. Add the carrots, red bell pepper, snow peas, baby corn, broccoli, and cauliflower. Cook for 5 to 6 minutes, stirring occasionally.
4. Add the cabbage and oyster sauce. Cook for another 3 minutes, stirring often.
5. Season with salt and pepper to taste. Remove from heat. Stir in sesame oil.
6. Transfer to a serving platter.
7. Serve and enjoy.

Spicy Water Spinach Stir Fry With Cashew

This is a very easy and a bit spicy vegetable dish that you can serve with grilled fish or poultry.

Preparation Time: 10 minutes
Total Time: 20 minutes
Yield: 4-6 servings

Ingredients
2 Tbsp. olive oil
1 medium red onion (chopped)
3 Tbsp. garlic (chopped)
2 lbs. water spinach (cut into 3 inch pieces, tough stems removed)
2 Tbsp. oyster sauce
2 Tbsp. chili garlic paste
1/2 cup dry roasted cashew nuts (coarsely ground)
salt and freshly ground black pepper

Method

1. Heat olive oil in a wok or large skillet over medium heat. Stir-fry onion and garlic for 3 minutes.
2. Add the water spinach, oyster sauce, and chili garlic paste. Cook, stirring from time to time, for about 5 to 7 minutes. Season with salt and pepper, to taste. Remove from heat.
3. Transfer to a serving platter. Sprinkle with cashew nuts.
4. Serve and enjoy.

Beef Veggie And Udon Stir Fry

This makes an awesome weeknight meal, it's complete with stir-fried beef, noodles and vegetables.

Preparation Time: 10 minutes
Total Time: 30 minutes
Yield: 4-6 servings

Ingredients
10 oz. udon noodles
2 Tbsp. vegetable oil
1/2 cup shallots (chopped)
2 cloves garlic (minced)
1 lb. sirloin beef (cut into thin strips)
4 oz. snap peas (trimmed)
1/2 tsp. Sichuan seasoning
1/3 cup tamari (wheat-free soy sauce)
1 Tbsp. sesame oil
salt and freshly ground black pepper

Method
1. Cook the udon noodles in a medium saucepan of boiling water for 8 to 10 minutes or until tender. Rinse under cold running water. Drain and set aside.
2. Heat the vegetable oil in a wok over medium-high heat. Stir-fry shallots and garlic for 3 minutes.
3. Add the beef and cook for about 7 minutes, stirring often.
4. Add the cooked noodles, snap peas, Sichuan seasoning, and tamari. Cook for another 3 minutes.
5. Stir in sesame oil. Season with salt and pepper to taste.
6. Transfer to a serving dish.
7. Serve and enjoy.

Bitter Melon With Tofu And Egg Stir-Fry

This healthy vegetable dish is rich in essential nutrients that promotes optimal health.

Preparation Time: 10 minutes
Total Time: 25 minutes
Yield: 6 servings

Ingredients
2 Tbsp. olive oil
1 (16 oz.) package firm tofu (cut into small cubes)
2 shallots onion (chopped)
3 cloves garlic (minced)
2 medium tomatoes (thinly sliced)
2 medium bitter melons
1 large egg (beaten)
salt and freshly ground black pepper

Method
1. Cut the bitter melons in half (lengthwise). Using a spoon, remove and discard the white part with the seeds. Slice thinly crosswise.
2. Heat olive oil in a non-stick fry pan over medium-high heat. Stir-fry onion, garlic, and tomatoes for 3 minutes.
3. Add the bitter melons. Cook, stirring frequently for about 7 to 10 minutes.
4. Stir in beaten egg. Cook for another 3 minute. Season with salt and pepper to taste.
5. Transfer in a serving dish.
6. Serve and enjoy.

Stir Fried Spicy Clams With Cilantro

This delightful seafood recipe is a must try if you!

Preparation Time: 8 hours 30 minutes
Total Time: 8 hours 30 minutes
Yield: 4 servings

Ingredients
1 lb. fresh clams
2 Tbsp. vegetable oil
2 shallots (chopped)
2 cloves garlic
1 tsp. fresh ginger root (finely chopped)
2 red chili peppers (thinly sliced)
2 Tbsp. cooking wine
2 Tbsp. cilantro (chopped)
salt and freshly ground black pepper

Method
1. Prepare a large bowl. Add enough water and 1 tablespoon of salt.

2. Place the clams in the salted water for at least 2 hours to remove the sands inside the clams.
3. Bring some water to a boil in a medium saucepan. Add clams and cook until they are slightly open. Remove from heat and drain.
4. Heat the vegetable oil in a wok over medium-high heat. Stir-fry shallots, garlic, ginger, chili peppers for 2 to 3 minutes.
5. Add the clams, wine, and cilantro. Cook further 2 to 3 minutes. Season with salt and pepper to taste.
6. Transfer to a serving dish.
7. Serve and enjoy.

Water Spinach And Tofu Stir-Fry With Garlic

This vegetable and tofu stir-fry recipe is bursting with amazing flavors and nutrition.

Preparation Time: 10 minutes
Total Time: 25 minutes
Yield: 6 servings

Ingredients
3 Tbsp. vegetable oil
1 (16 oz.) package firm tofu
1 medium onion (chopped)
1 lb. water spinach (cut into 2-inch pieces, large stems removed and)
1/4 Tbsp. Tamari
1/4 Tbsp. rice wine vinegar
1 tsp. brown sugar
2 Tbsp. toasted garlic bits
salt and freshly ground black pepper
toasted garlic

Method
1. In a large skillet, heat 2 tablespoons oil over medium-high heat. Cook the tofu until golden brown. Transfer to a plate and cut into small cubes. Set aside.
2. Using the same skillet, heat remaining oil. Stir-fry onion for 3 minutes.
3. Add the water spinach, Tamari, rice wine vinegar, and sugar. Cook for 5 minutes, stirring often.
4. Add the tofu and cook for another 2 to 3 minutes. Season with salt and pepper to taste.
5. Transfer to a serving dish Top with toasted garlic bits.
6. Serve and enjoy.

Shrimp Noodle Stir Fry With Scallion

This awesome shrimp and noodle stir-fry recipe makes a satisfying lunch or dinner.

Preparation Time: 15 minutes
Total Time: 30 minutes
Yield: 4-6 servings

Ingredients
2 Tbsp. vegetable oil
1 lb. fresh shrimps (peeled and deveined)
1/2 cup onion (chopped)
1 tsp. garlic (minced)
1 medium carrot (cut into thin strips)
2 cups vegetable stock (unsalted) or water
10 oz. chow mein noodles or dry egg noodles
1 small bunch scallions (cut into 2-inch pieces)
2 Tbsp. reduced-sodium soy sauce
1 Tbsp. Worcestershire sauce
salt and freshly ground black pepper

Method
1. Heat 1 tablespoon vegetable oil in a wok or skillet over medium-high heat. Stir-fry shrimps for 2 to 3 minutes. Transfer to a clean plate. Set aside.
2. In the same wok or skillet, heat remaining oil. Stir-fry onion and garlic for 3 minutes.
3. Add the carrot strips and cook for 3 to 5 minutes, stirring often.
4. Add the stock and bring to a boil.
5. Add the noodles, soy sauce, and Worcestershire sauce. Cook for about 7 to 8 minutes or until noodles are tender, stirring frequently.
6. Return the shrimps and add the scallions. Cook for another 2 minutes. Season with salt and pepper to taste. Remove from heat.
7. Transfer to a serving platter.
8. Serve and enjoy.

Vegetable Supreme Wok Stir-Fry

This colorful vegetable stir-fry recipe is not only pleasing to the eye, but tasty and healthy too!

Preparation Time: 10 minutes
Total Time: 25 minutes
Yield: 4-6 servings

Ingredients
2 Tbsp. olive oil
1 medium onion (chopped)
3 cloves garlic (minced)
2 cups broccoli florets
1 medium carrot (diced)
1 medium red bell pepper (deseeded and thinly sliced)
1 medium yellow bell pepper (deseeded and thinly sliced)
1 cup baby corn (cut into 1-inch pieces)
1 cup green beans (cut into 1-inch pieces)
1 cup canned sweet corn kernels (drained)
1/4 cup oyster sauce
salt and freshly ground black pepper

Method
1. Heat oil in a wok over medium-high heat. Stir-fry onion and garlic for 3 minutes.
2. Add the broccoli, carrot, bell peppers, baby corn, and green bean. Cook for about 8 minutes, stirring often.
3. Add the corn kernels and oyster sauce. Cook, stirring for another 2 to 3 minutes. Season with salt and pepper to taste. Remove from heat.
4. Transfer to a serving dish.
5. Serve and enjoy.

Lo Mein Chicken And Vegetable Stir Fry

This Asian noodle recipe is truly delicious and filling. It will make you crave for more!

Preparation Time: 10 minutes
Total Time: 30 minutes
Yield: 3-4 servings

Ingredients
2 Tbsp. vegetable oil
1/2 cup onion (chopped)
1 tsp. garlic (minced)
1 medium carrot (cut into thin strips)
1 cup cooked chicken breast (shredded)
2 cups chicken stock (unsalted) or water
10 oz. lo mein noodles or dry egg noodles
2 Tbsp. reduced-sodium soy sauce
1/4 cup green onions (chopped)
salt and freshly ground black pepper
1 medium lime (cut into wedges)

Method
1. Par-boil lo mein noodles in a saucepan with just enough water. Drain and set aside.
2. Heat vegetable oil in a wok or skillet over medium-high heat. Stir-fry onion and garlic for 3 minutes.
3. Add the carrot strips and shredded chicken. Cook for 3 to 5 minutes, stirring often.
4. Add the cooked noodles and soy sauce. Cook for about 5 to 7 minutes, stirring frequently. Season with salt and pepper to taste. Remove from heat.
5. Transfer to a serving platter. Sprinkle with fresh chives.
6. Serve with a slice of lime on the side.
7. Enjoy.

Shrimp And Chive Wok Stir-Fry

A super easy stir-fry recipe that needs only two main *ingredients*.

Preparation Time: 5 minutes
Total Time: 15 minutes
Yield: 4 servings

Ingredients
2 Tbsp. olive oil
1 lb. fresh shrimps (peeled and deveined)
1 bunch fresh chives (cut into 2-inch pieces)
1/2 tsp. garlic powder
1/2 tsp. ginger powder
salt and freshly ground black pepper

Method
1. Heat olive oil in a wok or skillet over medium-high heat.

2. Add the shrimps, chives, garlic powder, and ginger powder. Cook, stirring for 3 minutes or until shrimps turn pink. Season with salt and pepper to taste. Remove from heat.
3. Transfer to a serving platter.
4. Serve and enjoy.

Beef Wok Stir Fry With Mixed Veggies

This quickly stir-fried beef strips with a healthy mix of veggies make an awesome one-dish meal.

Preparation Time: 10 minutes
Total Time: 25 minutes
Yield: 6 servings

Ingredients
2 Tbsp. vegetable oil (divided)
1 lb. sirloin beef (thinly sliced)
1 medium onion (thinly sliced)
1 tsp. garlic (minced)
1 head broccoli (cut into small florets)
3 oz. green beans (trimmed and cut into 2-inch pieces)
1 medium carrot (thinly sliced)
1 head Chinese cabbage (cut into small pieces)
1/2 cup beef stock (unsalted)
2 Tbsp. soy sauce
salt and freshly ground black pepper

Method
1. Heat 1 tablespoon oil in a wok over medium-high heat. Stir-fry beef for 5 to 7 minutes or until browned. Transfer to a clean plate and cover to keep warm.
2. In the same wok, heat remaining oil. Stir-fry onion and garlic for 3 minutes.
3. Add the broccoli, green beans, and carrot. Cook, stirring for 5 minutes.
4. Return the beef into the wok. Add the Chinese cabbage, beef stock, and soy sauce. Cook for another 3 to 5 minutes, stirring often. Season with salt and pepper to taste.
5. Transfer to a serving dish.
6. Serve and enjoy.

Fresh Garden Vegetable Stir-Fry

This is one of the easiest and healthiest ways to prepare your vegetables.

Preparation Time: 10 minutes
Total Time: 20 minutes
Yield: 6 servings

Ingredients
2 Tbsp. olive oil
2 shallots (chopped)
3 Tbsp. olive oil
2 shallots (chopped)
1 tsp. garlic (minced)
1/2 tsp. fresh ginger root (grated)
1 head broccoli (cut into small florets)
1 medium zucchini (thinly sliced)
1 medium carrot (cut into thin strips)
1 medium red bell pepper (deseeded and thinly sliced)
1 medium yellow bell pepper (deseeded and thinly sliced)

1 cup button mushrooms (thinly sliced)
4 oz. green beans (trimmed and cut into 2-inch pieces)
salt and freshly ground black pepper

Method
1. Heat the olive oil in a wok or skillet over medium-high heat. Stir-fry shallots, garlic, and ginger for 3 minutes.
2. Add the broccoli, zucchini, carrot, bell peppers, mushrooms, green beans, and Worcestershire sauce. Cook, stirring for about 7 to 10 minutes or until crisp-tender. Season with salt and pepper, to taste.
3. Transfer to a serving dish.
4. Serve and enjoy.

Chicken Zucchini And Eggplant Stir Fry

Enjoy this chicken stir-fry with zucchini, eggplant, and tomatoes over steamed rice.

Preparation Time: 10 minutes
Total Time: 30 minutes
Yield: 6 servings

Ingredients
3 Tbsp. vegetable oil
1 medium red onion (chopped)
1 tsp. garlic (minced)
2 medium tomatoes (diced))
1 lb. chicken breast fillet (cut into 1-inch cubes)
1 medium zucchini (diced)
1 medium eggplant (diced)
2/3 cup chicken stock (reduced-sodium)
salt and freshly ground black pepper

Method
1. Heat 1 tablespoon oil in a large skillet or wok over medium-high heat. Stir-fry chicken for 7 to 8

minutes or until browned. Transfer to a clean plate and cover to keep warm. Set aside.
2. Heat remaining oil in the same skillet. Stir-fry onion and garlic for 3 minutes.
3. Add the tomatoes, zucchini, and eggplant. Cook for 8 minutes, stirring often.
4. Return chicken into the skillet and add the chicken stock. Cook for another 5 to 7 minutes, stirring occasionally. Season with salt and pepper to taste.
5. Transfer to a serving dish.
6. Serve and enjoy.

Shrimp And Broccoli Stir-Fry Asian-Style

Try this awesome stir-fried shrimps with broccoli has a perfect blend of Asian flavors that you will surely love.

Preparation Time: 10 minutes
Total Time: 25 minutes
Yield: 4 servings

Ingredients
3 Tbsp. peanut oil
2 shallots (chopped)
1 tsp. garlic (minced)
1 tsp. fresh ginger root (grated)
1 lb. fresh shrimp (peeled and deveined)
1 head broccoli (cut into small florets)
2/3 cup vegetable stock (unsalted)
2 tsp. sesame oil
salt and freshly ground black pepper

Method

1. Heat 1 tablespoon peanut oil in a large skillet or wok over medium heat. Cook the shrimps for 3 minutes. Transfer to a clean plate and set aside.
2. In the same skillet or wok, heat the remaining oil. Stir-fry the shallots, garlic, and ginger for 3 minutes.
3. Add the broccoli and cook, stirring for 5 minutes.
4. Add the vegetable stock and cook further 5 minutes or until the broccoli is crisp-tender.
5. Stir in sesame oil. Season with salt and pepper, to taste. Remove from heat.
6. Transfer to a serving dish.
7. Serve and enjoy.

Chow Mein Noodles With Chicken

This delightful Asian noodle dish with chicken and vegetables is a hit!

Preparation Time: 10 minutes
Total Time: 30 minutes
Yield: 4-6 servings

Ingredients
2 Tbsp. peanut oil
12 oz. chicken breast (cut into thin strips)
1/2 cup white onion (chopped)
3 cloves garlic (crushed)
1 medium carrot (cut into thin strips)
2 stalks celery (diced)
1 cup chicken stock
1 cup water
2 Tbsp. oyster sauce
10 oz. Chow Mein noodles (dry)
1/4 cup leeks (thinly sliced)
1/4 cilantro (chopped)

salt and freshly ground black pepper

Method
1. Heat peanut oil in a wok over medium-high heat. Stir-fry onion and garlic for 3 minutes.
2. Add chicken and cook for about 7 minutes.
3. Add carrot strips and celery. Cook, stirring for 3 to 5 minutes.
4. Add chicken stock, water, and oyster sauce. Bring to a boil.
5. Add the egg noodles and cook until almost tender.
6. Add the leeks and cilantro. Cook for another 3-5 minutes, stirring often. Season with salt and pepper to taste. Turn off heat.
7. Transfer to a serving platter.
8. Serve and enjoy.

Soy Chicken And Mushroom Stir Fry

Try this simple yet super delicious recipe tonight!

Preparation Time: 10 minutes
Total Time: 25 minutes
Yield: 4 servings

Ingredients
2 Tbsp. vegetable oil
1/2 cup scallions (chopped)
2 cloves garlic, minced
1/2 tsp. ginger (minced)
1 lb. chicken breast fillet (thinly sliced)
2 cups button mushrooms (sliced)
1/4 cup soy sauce (reduced-sodium)
2 tsp. Worcestershire sauce
1 tsp. brown sugar
salt and freshly ground black pepper
fresh parsley

Method

1. In a wok or large skillet, heat vegetable oil over medium-high heat. Stir-fry scallions, garlic, and ginger for 2 to 3 minutes.
2. Add the chicken and mushrooms. Cook, stirring for 7 minutes.
3. Add the soy sauce, Worcestershire sauce, and brown sugar. Cook for another 5 minutes, stirring frequently. Season with salt and pepper, to taste. Turn off heat.
4. Transfer to a serving dish. Garnish with fresh parsley or scallions.
5. Serve and enjoy.

Stir-Fried Vegetables With Shiitake And Tofu

Try this wonderful vegetable dish it is perfect for a quick lunch or dinner!

Preparation Time: 10 minutes
Total Time: 25 minutes
Yield: 4 servings

Ingredients
2 Tbsp. vegetable oil
1 medium red onion (chopped)
1 tsp. garlic (minced)
1 medium carrot (thinly sliced)
1 head cauliflower (cut into small florets)
1 cup shiitake mushrooms (thinly sliced)
1 cup snap peas (trimmed)
1 head cabbage (shredded)
8 oz. firm tofu (cut into 1-inch cubes)
2/3 cup chicken stock
1/4 cup chives (chopped)
salt and freshly ground black pepper

Method
1. In a wok or large skillet, heat vegetable oil over medium-high heat. Stir-fry onion and garlic for 3 minutes.
2. Add the carrot, shiitake mushrooms, and snap peas. Cook for about 5 minutes, stirring frequently.
3. Add the cabbage, tofu, chicken stock, and chives. Cook further 3 to 5 minutes. Season with salt and pepper, to taste. Turn off heat.
4. Transfer to a serving dish.
5. Serve and enjoy.

String Bean Stir Fry With Holy Basil

This vegetable stir-fry makes a great side dish to grilled fish or poultry.

Preparation Time: 5 minutes
Total Time: 15 minutes
Yield: 4 servings

Ingredients
1 Tbsp. vegetable oil
1 large red onion (thinly sliced)
1 tsp. garlic (minced)
1 lb. string beans (trimmed and cut into 2-inch pieces)
1/2 cup blackbean sauce
1 Tbsp. fish sauce
1/2 cup holy basil (leaves separated)
salt and freshly ground black pepper

Method
1. In a wok or large skillet, heat vegetable oil over medium-high heat. Stir-fry red onion and garlic for 3 minutes.
2. Add the string beans, black bean sauce, and fish sauce. Cook for about 7 to 8 minutes, stirring frequently.
3. Add the holy basil and cook further 3 minutes. Season with salt and pepper, to taste. Turn off heat.
4. Transfer to a serving dish.
5. Serve and enjoy.

Chicken Pepper And Leek Stir Fry

A very delicious and easy to prepare dish in less than 30 minutes!

Preparation Time: 10 minutes
Total Time: 25 minutes
Yield: 4 servings

Ingredients
2 Tbsp. vegetable oil
1 tsp. garlic (minced)
1 lb. chicken breast fillet (cut into strips)
1 medium red bell pepper carrots (cut into strips)
1 medium yellow bell pepper carrots (cut into strips)
1/4 cup Sichuan sauce
2 leeks (thinly sliced)
1 tsp. sesame oil
salt and freshly ground black pepper
toasted sesame seeds

Method
1. Heat vegetable oil in a wok over medium-high heat. Stir-fry garlic for 2 minutes.
2. Add the chicken strips. Cook, stirring frequently for about 8 minutes.
3. Add the bell peppers and Sichuan sauce. Cook for another 5 minutes.
4. Stir in leeks and sesame oil. Season with salt and pepper, to taste. Remove from heat.
5. Transfer to a serving dish. Sprinkle with toasted sesame seeds.
6. Serve and enjoy.

Vegetarian Noodle Stir-Fry

This Vegetarian-friendly noodle stir-fry is yummy and very easy to prepare!

Preparation Time: 10 minutes
Total Time: 10 minutes
Yield: 4 servings

Ingredients
2 Tbsp. peanut oil
1 medium red onion (chopped)
1 tsp. garlic (minced)
1 medium carrot (cut into thin strips)
1 cup green beans (trimmed and cut into 1-inch pieces)
1 medium red bell pepper (deseeded and cut into strips)
1 stalk celery (diced)
2 cups vegetable stock (unsalted)
1 cup water
1/4 cup Tamari
10 oz. egg noodles (dry)
2 cups mungbean sprouts

2 Tbsp. cilantro (chopped)
1/2 cup coarsely chopped cashew nuts
salt and freshly ground black pepper

Method
1. Heat peanut oil in a wok over medium-high heat. Stir-fry onion and garlic for 5 minutes.
2. Add the carrot, green beans, red bell pepper, and celery. Cook, stirring for 3 minutes.
3. Add vegetable stock, water, and Tamari. Bring to a boil over high heat.
4. Add the egg noodles and cook, stirring occasionally until almost tender.
5. Add the mungbean sprouts and cilantro. Cook further 3 minutes, stirring often. Season with pepper to taste. Remove from heat.
6. Transfer to a serving dish. Sprinkle with cashew nuts.
7. Serve and enjoy.

Part 2

Introduction

Stir frying is one of the most used cooking methods all over the world. Not only that it's easy to do, it's fast, convenient and you can use it on any ingredients that are available at hand.

Stir frying is a popular cooking technique by the Chinese. It was first introduced in China because they work fast and efficiently on brick stoves that Chinese have on their home. Usually a simple wok with a curved, broad spatula is needed to do this cooking method.

This method is simple and easy. Chopped food and oil are tossed and stirred on the pan, cooking your ingredients fast and served hot. One great thing about stir frying is that ingredients remain fresh, hot and colors remain vibrant. This is because food is cooked quickly on high heat resulting to flavors being preserved and contained on the dish.

So, come on and enjoy these delicious and succulent stir fry recipes I've prepared for you. Not only that it's fast and convenient but healthy too. Put on your apron and cooking hat and let's start cooking!

1. Pork Teriyaki Don

Pork tenderloins are good cuts of meat that you can use for this dish. Not only that it's lean and tender but it also cooks really fast.

Ingredients

- ½ cup of soy sauce
- ½ cup of mirin
- 3 tablespoons of sugar
- ½ teaspoon of ginger (grated)
- 350 grams of pork (tenderloins; cut to strips)
- 2 tablespoons of oil
- ¼ teaspoon of sesame oil
- 1 bell pepper (diced, can use green or red)
- Cooked rice for serving

Method

1. Combine soy sauce, sugar, mirin and ginger in a bowl. Add pork strips and toss it to evenly coat. Cover and cool in refrigerator for about 20 minutes.
2. Heat oil over medium to high heat inside a wok. Stir fry marinated pork for 1 minute then transfer on a plate. Set aside.
3. Pour on sesame oil and sauté the bell peppers. Put back the pork with the marinade and cook until done. Season to taste. Serve on top of cooked rice. Enjoy!

Tips

You can marinate your pork a night before cooking. That way flavors are more absorbed and infused on the meat itself.

2. Healthy Beef Broccoli Stir Fry

Tender, melt in your mouth beefy goodness paired with vibrant and crunchy broccoli is a surefire hit for your friends and family. Quick, easy and healthy – an all-time dish in a jiffy.

Ingredients

For the beef
- 300 grams of beef sirloin (sliced to 2x1 inches)
- ½ teaspoon of meat tenderizer
- 1 tablespoon of soy sauce
- 2 tablespoons of ginger juice
- ¼ teaspoon of salt
- A pinch of pepper
- 1 tablespoon of egg white
- 1 tablespoon of cornstarch
- 1 cup of cooking oil

For the broccoli

- 1 medium sized broccoli
- 1 tablespoon of oil
- 1 teaspoon of garlic

For stir frying

- 2 tablespoons of oil
- 1 piece of small ginger (pounded)
- 1 tablespoon of garlic (chopped)
- 1 stalk of leek (sliced to an inch-thick rings)
- 5 slices of carrots
- 12 pieces of snow peas
- 2 tablespoons of oyster sauce
- 2 tablespoons of gin
- ½ cup of chicken stock
- 1 tablespoon of cornstarch (dissolve it on 2 tablespoons of water)
- 1 tablespoon of sesame oil
- Salt, sugar and pepper for tasting

Method

1. To prepare the beef: mix beef and the meat tenderizer and let rest for about 5 minutes. Add soy sauce, salt, ginger juice and pepper. Marinate it the whole night.
2. Once you are ready to prepare the dish, mix the cornstarch and egg white to the meat. Heat oil inside the wok and start frying the beef for approximately 3 minutes. Set aside.

3. To prepare the broccoli: blanch it over boiling water until color changes. Place in a bowl of ice water to maintain crunchiness of veggie. Heat oil in a pan and sauté the garlic until fragrant. Add broccoli and mix them well. Transfer to a plate and set them aside.
4. Heat oil in the wok. Sauté ginger and garlic until it becomes fragrant. Mix in all other veggies, gin, oyster sauce and stock. Once it boils, add beef and continue to cook. Season to taste using sugar, pepper and salt. Use the cornstarch mixture to thicken the sauce. Once done add sesame oil.
5. Pour the cooked mixture on top of the broccoli and serve. Enjoy!

Tips

To make the ginger juice, peel a small sized ginger and grate. Squeeze the grated ginger to get the juice and strain. This would make 2 tablespoons of ginger juice.

3. Tenderloin Strips With Lemongrass

Are you in a hurry? Then stir frying is the best way to cook quick and healthy meals. Try this low-fat and protein packed recipe that is perfect for people in a hurry. Infused with cilantro and lemongrass, you will definitely enjoy the hint of Thai flavor.

Ingredients

- 1 ½ tablespoons of brown sugar
- 1 tablespoon of KecapManis (sweet soy sauce)
- 1 tablespoon of fish sauce
- ½ teaspoon of salt
- ¼ teaspoon of pepper
- 400 grams of beef tenderloin (sliced to 2 ½ inch thick strips)
- 1 tablespoon of cornstarch
- 2 tablespoons of cooking oil
- 1 medium sized red onions (thinly sliced)

- 2 teaspoons of garlic (chopped finely)
- 5 stalks of lemongrass (minced and trimed)
- 1-2 pieces of bird's eye chili (chopped)
- 3 tablespoons of cilantro (chopped)
- Steamed rice for serving

Method

1. In a medium sized bowl, mix together kecapmanis, sugar, fish sauce, pepper and salt. Add the tenderloin strips and mix them well. Sprinkle it with cornstarch and combine them well. Marinate for about 15 minutes or if possible, do it overnight.
2. Heat the oil in a large sized wok over medium to high heat then sauté onions until cooked. Add the lemongrass and garlic and continue sautéing until they are fragrant. Add the beef with the marinade. Stir fry around 5-6 minutes or until beef is done depending on your preference.
3. Add the chilies and stir continuously for a few seconds. Remove from heat and add the chopped cilantro. Mix it well. Serve immediately with the steamed rice and top it with cilantro leaves as garnish. Enjoy!

Tips

KecapManis is a sweet soy sauce used mostly in Indonesia and other Asian countries. It is thick, not salty and have rich caramel flavor. They are available on groceries and supermarkets.

4. Beef Stir Fry With Long Beans & Aromatic Paste

Now let me take you to the flavors of Thailand. A sumptuous and fragrant dish, this would liven up your palate and let you discover new and bold flavors.

Ingredients

- 2 tablespoons of oyster sauce
- 2 tablespoons of sugar (dark brown or you can use muscovado sugar if available)
- 1 tablespoon of fish sauce
- 350 grams of beef tenderloin (sliced to thin strips)

To prepare aromatic paste

- 1 stalk of lemongrass (minced and trimmed)
- 3 tablespoons of shallot (minced)
- 2 tablespoons of garlic (minced)
- 1 tablespoon of cilantro (minced)

- 2 teaspoons of Thai shrimp paste
- 1 teaspoon of ginger
- ½ teaspoon of chili flakes (optional)
- 5 pieces of black peppercorns
- 1 teaspoon of salt
- 3 tablespoons of vegetable oil
- 150 grams of string beans (cut into 1½ inch long, blanced)
- Pepper and salt for tasting
- 1-2 pieces of leaves of Kaffir lime (leaves thinly sliced; ribs discarded)
- Steamed rice (optional)

Method

1. In a medium sized bowl, make the marinade. Combine sugar, oyster sauce and fish sauce. Mix well until sugar is fully dissolved. Add the beef and marinate for about 3-6 hours. But it's still best to marinate it overnight.
2. To make the aromatic paste, mix all of the ingredients in a large sized pestle and mortar. Pound the ingredients until achieving a smooth paste texture.
3. In a medium sized wok, heat the oil then sauté the aromatic paste for about a minute until fragrant. Add beef and its marinade and cook over medium high heat until the beef is cooked well and browned.

4. Add the blanched string beans and stir well. Season to taste then add the leaves of Kaffir lime. Remove from heat. Serve with rice if you want. Enjoy!

Tips and notes

String beans are also called yard beans. They are a good source of folates and also have a good amount of Vitamin C that is good for the body.

5. Stir-Fried Veggie Egg Noodles With Pork

This is an appetizing noodle dish that would surely be a hit when you have visitors at home. It's quick and easy to prepare, easy on the budget and healthy for the body.

Ingredients

- 200 grams of egg noodles
- 1 tablespoon of canola oil
- 2 cloves of garlic (finely chopped)
- 100 grams of pork belly (sliced thinly and no skins)
- ½ cup leeks (thinly sliced, white part only)
- 2 tablespoons of cooking wine (Chinese variety)
- 1 cup of straw mushrooms (canned, drained and cut to half)
- 2 tablespoons of green onions (chopped)
- 2 tablespoons of cilantro

For the sauce

- 1 ½ tablespoons of oyster sauce
- 2 teaspoons of soy sauce
- 1 teaspoon of sugar
- 1 teaspoon of sesame oil
- Pepper and salt for tasting
- ½ cup of chicken stock or water if not available

Method

1. Put 4 cups of water in the wok. Bring to boil. Blanch the noodles in the boiling water for about 30 seconds to a minute then drain. Run through cold water and shake excess water.
2. To make the sauce: mix all the ingredients until sugar is well dissolved.
3. Using same wok, heat oil over medium to high heat. Sauté garlic and add the pork belly. Stir fry until it turned light brown. Add cooking wine and leeks, stir well. Remove and set aside.
4. Pour the sauce and simmer over medium-high heat. Add pork mixture, mushrooms and noodles. Toss continuously to prevent from sticking on the wok. Stir well to coat the noodles evenly. Turn the heat off and add cilantro and green onions. Serve hot and enjoy!

Tips

You can substitute pork with chicken for a much healthier meat choice and lower calorie meal.

6. Stir-Fried Vegetables Chinese Style

A delicious and colorful dish filled with healthy vegetables that are easy to cook in a jiffy.

Ingredients

- 2 tablespoons of vegetable oil
- ½ cup of red onion (sliced thinly)
- 200 grams of skinless pork belly (thinly sliced to an inch per piece
- 1 small sized zucchini (sliced into round sizes)
- 1 cup of cauliflower
- 1 medium sized carrots (sliced into round sizes)
- 1 eggplant (cut to an inch)
- 1 cup bell pepper (sliced)
- 1 clove garlic (minced)
- 1 teaspoon ginger (minced)
- ½ cup of oyster sauce

- 1 tablespoon of sugar (dissolve it in 2 tablespoons of water)
- 1 cup of green beans (trimmed)
- ¼ teaspoon of black pepper (ground)
- ¼ teaspoon of salt
- 2 tablespoons of sesame oil

Method

1. In a large size wok, heat oil over medium to high heat. Add the onions and stir continuously then add the pork until browned. Add in the zucchini, carrots, cauliflower, bell pepper, eggplant, ginger, garlic and oyster sauce.
2. Pour the sugar mixture and stir continuously. Cook for about 2 minutes. Add the beans, salt and pepper for tasting. Cook well. Once done turn off heat then pour some sesame oil. Serve hot and enjoy!

Tips

Make sure to prep all your veggies ahead before cooking so can you can cook it quicker and faster.

7. Stir Fried Vermicelli With Chicken Teriyaki

This is a complete meal that you would surely go back for more. Packed with proteins, carbohydrates and energy boosting ingredients, this would definitely satisfy any health-conscious individual.

Ingredients

- 500 grams of chicken fillet (breast part; cut into strips)

For the Teriyaki sauce

- 8 tablespoons of soy sauce (Japanese style)

- 2 tablespoons of sake (rice wine)
- 4 tablespoons of water
- 1 tablespoon of brown sugar
- 4 tablespoons of white sugar
- 1 ½ teaspoon of garlic (chopped finely)
- 11/2 teaspoon of ginger (grated)

For the vermicelli noodles

- 200 grams of vermicelli noodles
- 1 liter of boiling water
- 1 tablespoon of sesame oil
- 250 grams of snow peas (remove strings)
- 200 grams of red cabbage (shredded)
- 1 teaspoon of garlic (chopped finely)
- 1 tablespoon of hoisin sauce
- 1 tablespoon of soy sauce (light variety)
- 2 tablespoons of water
- Ground black pepper
- Sesame seeds (if desired)

Method

1. Prepare the teriyaki sauce by combining all the ingredients. Make sure to mix them all well. Once done, place the chicken strips and marinate for 1-3 hours.
2. Start cooking vermicelli noodles by putting them on a heat-resistant bowl and adding boiling water. Soak and cover noodles for about 3-5 minutes. Using the fork, separate noodles, drain and set aside.
3. To cook chicken, heat the grill to high. Spread a few oil and grill chicken for about 5 minutes. Brush the chicken with the marinade on both sides while cooking. Once done, put them on a plate and set aside.

4. In a large sized wok, heat oil over medium to high heat. Add garlic with the red cabbage and stir fry for about 2 minutes. Add hoisin sauce, water, soy sauce and cook for about 1-2 minutes.
5. Put snow peas and simmer until it becomes crisp and light green. Add noodles and toss to evenly spread the flavors. Once done transfer to plate. Place the grilled chicken on top of the noodles. If desired, sprinkle some sesame seeds. Serve hot and enjoy!

Tips

Vermicelli noodles are thin forms of rice noodles. They are used commonly as stir fried for Pad Thai, toppings on salads or soups like Vietnamese Pho. They are cholesterol free, fat free and has low sodium content.

8. Shrimp Chili Stir Fry

If you are a fan of food with a bit of heat, try this fast and delicious shrimp recipe to liven up the palates. Best with wine or a few beers with some friends on a Super Bowl or Boxing night.

Ingredients

- 300 grams of shrimp (deveined and shelled)
- 1 tablespoon of soy sauce (light variety)
- 2 tablespoons of oil
- 1 tablespoon of onion (chopped)
- 1 tablespoon of garlic (chopped)
- 2 pieces of bird's eye chili (chopped)
- 1/3 cup of bell pepper, red (cubed)
- 1/3 cup of bell pepper, green (cubed)
- 1/3 cup of bell pepper, yellow (cubed)
- 1 stalk of leeks (shredded)

To prepare the sauce

- 1 tablespoon of chili-garlic sauce
- 1 tablespoon of oyster sauce
- 1 tablespoon of gin
- ½ cup of chicken stock
- 1 tablespoon of water
- 1 tablespoon of cornstarch dissolved in 2 teaspoons of water
- 1 tablespoon of sesame oil

Method

1. Marinate the shrimp in salt, soy sauce and pepper. Put inside the refrigerator.
2. To prep the sauce, combine all the ingredients and mix well. Set aside.
3. In a wok, stir fry the onions, chili and garlic. Add shrimps and the bell peppers. When the shrimp starts curling and turning orange, pour the sauce. Season with pepper, sugar and salt. Thicken it with the cornstarch mixture and add some sesame oil. Remove from heat. Serve with shredded leeks on top. Enjoy!

Tips

It's always best to buy the shrimps on the day you will be cooking them because the fresher the *ingredients*, the better!

9. Chicken Rice Indian Style

Expand and try out these other fried rice varieties using exotic and fragrant Indian spices. You will surely love them!

Ingredients

- 2 tablespoons of butter (unsalted)
- 2 tablespoons of onion (chopped)
- 1 teaspoon of garlic (minced)
- 2 pieces of chicken breast (fillet part, cubed)
- ½ teaspoon of cumin (ground)
- 2 teaspoon of curry powder
- 1 teaspoon of turmeric (ground)
- ¼ cup of frozen peas
- ¼ cup of raisins
- 4 cups of brown rice (cooked; you can also use red rice)

- Pepper and salt for tasting
- 3 tablespoons of almonds (slivered and toasted)

Method

1. Heat the butter and sauté the garlic and onions. Add the chicken and cook thoroughly. Add curry powder, cumin and turmeric. Mix them well.
2. Add peas and raisins then combine it with the cooked rice and stir fry until well coated with the spices. Season to taste. Once done remove from heat. Put in serving bowls and top it with almonds. Serve hot and enjoy!

Tips

This rice bowl will go perfectly with other grilled meats or vegetables.

10. Quick Stir-Fried Water Spinach With Pork Rind

A tasty vegetable dish with a few indulgent pork cracklings for added crunch and exciting flavors.

Ingredients

- 5 teaspoons of oil
- 2 teaspoons of garlic (minced)
- 2 tablespoons of shrimp paste
- 300 grams of water spinach (separate leaves and stem)
- 4 teaspoons of vinegar
- 2 teaspoons of water
- 2 pieces of pork rind (crumbled)

Method

1. Heat the oil and sauté garlic in a medium sized wok or pan. Add shrimp paste and stir fry for a minute.

2. Add water spinach stems and cook until turned bright green in color. Add the leaves and cook it until it is wilted.
3. Pour the water and vinegar. Bring to boil and remove from fire. Transfer the veggies to a plate and top it with crumbled pork rind. Serve and enjoy.

Tips

Pork rinds are often called "chicharon" – a crispy pork crackling that are packed and can be readily bought in specialty supermarkets or Asian stores. If you can't find these pork rinds, you can substitute it with any crispy chicken skins or bacon that you can make on your own.

11. Brown Rice With Stir-Fried Beef Teriyaki

Here's another rice dish that you can check out. Healthy, quick and a good idea for people on the go.

Ingredients

- 2 teaspoons of cornstarch
- 3 tablespoons of teriyaki sauce
- 4 tablespoons of olive oil
- 500 grams of beef tenderloin (cut to thinly sliced strips)
- ½ cup of carrots (diced)
- ¼ cup green beans (blanched)
- 1 cup of baby corn (boiled)
- 3 cups of brown rice (cooked)

Method

1. Combine teriyaki sauce, cornstarch and 2 tablespoons of oil in a small sized bowl. Add beef

and marinate it for about 45 minutes. Put it inside the refrigerator.
2. In a medium sized pan, stir fry green beans, baby corn and carrots with the remaining oil for about 2-3 minutes. Transfer on a plate.
3. Using the same pan, stir-fry the beef for about 3 minutes until it is tender. Bring back the vegetables and continue to stir fry for another 1-2 minutes. Remove from heat. Serve over the cooked rice and enjoy!

Tips

In this dish you may also use the sukiyaki cut beef instead of the beef tenderloin.

12. Two Sauce Pork Tenders Stir Fry

This is one dish that will gratify two tastes – one with a creamy mushroom sauce and the other spicy and sweet for a little kick on the palate!

Ingredients

For the pork tenders

- 1 ½ table spoons of oil
- 2 teaspoons of garlic powder
- 2 teaspoons of onion powder
- 1 ½ teaspoons of soy sauce
- 1 kilo of pork tenderloin (sliced to ¼ inch size)

To prepare sweet & spicy sauce

- 2 tablespoons of oil
- 1 tablespoon of garlic (minced)
- 1 onion (sliced)

- 1 red bell pepper (sliced)
- 1 green bell pepper (sliced)
- ½ cup of sweet chili sauce
- A dash of cayenne pepper

To prepare mushroom sauce

- ¼ cup of butter
- 1 teaspoon of garlic (minced)
- 1 small size canned mushrooms (sliced)
- 1 bottle of prepared gravy
- 1 teaspoon of Worcestershire sauce
- ½ teaspoon of soy sauce

Method

1. To prepare pork tenders: combine all the ingredients in a medium sized bowl and place the pork tenders on it. Marinate for about 15 minutes and divide it to 2 portions. Set aside.
2. To prepare the sweet & spicy sauce: heat oil in wok and sauté the onion and garlic. Add bell peppers and half of the marinated pork tenders. Stir fry until the pork is cooked thoroughly. Pour the sweet chili sauce and a dash of cayenne pepper and salt. You can adjust the heat depending on your taste.
3. To prepare the mushroom sauce: Melt butter on a different pan and sauté garlic. Add the rest of the pork tenders and cook well. Stir in gravy and mushrooms and bring to boil. Season with

Worcestershire sauce and soy sauce. Simmer until cooked thoroughly. Prepare cooked rice in a bowl. Top it with preferred sauce and you are good to go. Enjoy!

Tips

The bottle of gravy in this recipe can be replaced using the canned cream of mushroom. Just use half of it and mix with a few cups of water and you will be able to prepare a creamy mushroom sauce.

13. Bell Pepper And Squid Stir Fry

This easy squid stir fry can also be used as a perfect topping for your egg noodles or rice meal.

Ingredients

- 1 kilo of squid
- 1 tablespoon of hot bean paste
- 2 tablespoons of soy sauce
- 1 tablespoon of rice wine
- 2 teaspoons of sesame oil
- 1 teaspoon of salt
- 1 tablespoon of oil
- 2 tablespoons of garlic (minced)
- 1 teaspoon of garlic (minced)
- 1/3 cup of bell pepper, red (sliced to strips)
- 1/3 cup of bell pepper, green (sliced to strips)
- 1/3 cup of bell pepper, yellow (sliced to strips)
- Toasted sesame seeds

Method

1. Clean the squid, separate the heads from their bodies. Set aside and keep the squid heads. Peel the skin off their bodies and wash well. Score each squid and make a crisscross pattern on the body. Cut for about 2x2 inch squares. In a small saucepan, bring water to a boil. Drop the squid and let it boil once again. Quickly remove the squid and set aside.
2. In a medium sized bowl, mix hot bean paste, rice wine, soy sauce, salt and sesame oil. Set aside. Heat the wok and add oil. Sauté ginger and garlic. Add bell pepper strips and squid. Stir fry for about a minute then add the hot bean paste. Simmer for a few minutes. Serve hot and top it with cilantro and toasted sesame seeds. Enjoy!

Tips

When scoring, use a thin, sharp knife to make those cuts. Make sure that you don't cut through the squid meat.

14. Thai-Style Prawn Salad

Another Asian inspired cuisine that captures the taste of Thailand. You can serve this dish either hot or cold – any which way, it's delicious!

Ingredients

- 200 grams of vermicelli noodles
- 1 tablespoon of oil
- 2 cloves of garlic (chopped)
- 1 piece of ginger (finely chopped)
- 1 piece of bird's eye chili (seeded, finely chopped)
- 450 grams of prawns (peeled, deveined, tails intact)
- 2 cups of snow peas
- 8 pieces of baby corn (halved in lengthwise)
- 4 stalks of spring onions (thinly sliced)
- 1 tablespoon of sesame seeds (toasted)
- 1 stalk of lemongrass (shredded thinly)

Dressing preparation

- 1 tablespoon of spring onions (chopped)
- 1 tablespoon of fish sauce
- 1 teaspoon of soy sauce
- 3 tablespoons of oil
- 1 teaspoon of sesame oil
- 2 tablespoons of rice vinegar

Method

1. Place the noodles in a large sized bowl. Pour boiling water over until fully immersed. Soak for about 5 minutes. Drain the noodles and refresh in cold water. Drain and set aside.
2. In a bottle or a bowl, mix all the ingredients for the dressing and combine them well. In a medium sized wok or pan, heat oil and sauté garlic, chili and ginger. Add the prawns. Cook for about 3 minutes until it changes in color.
3. Stir in the snow peas, spring onions, sesame seed and baby corn. Toss it lightly and mix well. Arrange the drained noodles in a serving plate. Top it with the cooked prawns. Drizzle with the prepared dressing. Serve and garnish with shredded lemon grass. Enjoy!

Tips

The quickest way in making vinaigrette is to put all *ingredients* in a bottle, tightly cover it and shake it well.

By keeping it in a bottle, you can easily use it again for other salad dishes.

15. Fried Rice Oriental

This fried rice is packed with veggies and meat that makes it a complete, satisfying meal by itself.

Ingredients

- 2 tablespoons of oil
- 1 tablespoon of garlic (chopped)
- 1 onion (chopped)
- 500 grams of ground chicken
- 2 pieces of chorizo (Chinese style, minced)
- 1 cup of mixed vegetables (frozen packed)
- 1 tablespoon of garlic chili sauce
- 3 tablespoons of soy sauce
- 4 tablespoons of hoisin sauce
- 6 cups of rice (cooked)
- Sugar, pepper and salt for tasting
- 1 teaspoon of sesame oil

Method

1. Heat the oil in a medium sized wok. Sauté onions and the garlic. Add chorizos and ground chicken. Stir fry until chicken is cooked. Add in the vegetables.
2. Season with the garlic chili sauce, hoisin and soy sauce. Add cooked rice. Mix well until evenly coated. Season according to your preferred taste. Drizzle with the sesame season. Serve hot and enjoy!

Tips

You can make a seafood variation by substituting chicken and chorizo with shrimps, crabmeat and squid.

16. Beef Stir Fry With Long Beans & Aromatic Paste

Now let me take you to the flavors of Thailand. A sumptuous and fragrant dish, this would liven up your palate and let you discover new and bold flavors.

Ingredients

- 2 tablespoons of oyster sauce
- 2 tablespoons of sugar (dark brown or you can use muscovado sugar if available)
- 1 tablespoon of fish sauce
- 350 grams of beef tenderloin (sliced to thin strips)
- 1 stalk of lemongrass (minced and trimmed)
- 3 tablespoons of shallot (minced)
- 2 tablespoons of garlic (minced)
- 1 tablespoon of cilantro (minced)
- 2 teaspoons of Thai shrimp paste
- 1 teaspoon of ginger
- ½ teaspoon of chili flakes (optional)
- 5 pieces of black peppercorns

- 1 teaspoon of salt
- 3 tablespoons of vegetable oil
- 150 grams of string beans (cut into 1½ inch long, blanced)
- Pepper and salt for tasting
- 1-2 pieces of leaves of Kaffir lime (leaves thinly sliced; ribs discarded)
- Steamed rice (optional)

Method

1. In a medium sized bowl, make the marinade. Combine sugar, oyster sauce and fish sauce. Mix well until sugar is fully dissolved. Add the beef and marinate for about 3-6 hours. But it's still best to marinate it overnight.
2. To make the aromatic paste, mix all of the ingredients in a large sized pestle and mortar. Pound the ingredients until achieving a smooth paste texture.
3. In a medium sized wok, heat the oil then sauté the aromatic paste for about a minute until fragrant. Add beef and its marinade and cook over medium high heat until the beef is cooked well and browned. Add the blanched string beans and stir well. Season to taste then add the leaves of Kaffir lime. Remove from heat.

17. Thai Squash Curry

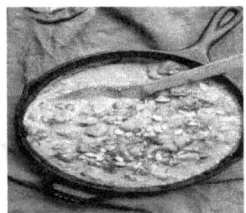

The Thai red curry paste gives this dish a spicy kick!

Serves: 6
Time to Prepare: 20 min

Ingredients

- 1 lb Chopped Firm Tofu
- 1 Chopped Butternut Squash
- 1 Tbsp Vegetable Oil
- 1 Sliced Onion
- 2 Minced Garlic Cloves
- 2 Tsp Thai Red Curry Paste
- 14 oz Light Coconut Milk
- 1/2 cup Vegetable Stock
- 2 Tbsp Soy Sauce
- 1 Tbsp Packed Brown Sugar
- 1 Tbsp Fish Sauce
- 1/2 Tsp Salt
- 1 Sliced Red Pepper

- 1/4 cup Chopped Fresh Cilantro
- 2 Tbsp Lime Juice
- 2 Tbsp Chopped Salted Peanuts

Method

1. In a wok or large frying pan, add oil, minced garlic, curry paste, & sliced onion. Sauté for 5 minutes. Add chopped squash, light coconut milk, vegetable stock, soy sauce, sugar, fish sauce, & salt.
2. Bring to a boil before reducing heat for 12 minutes. Add sliced red pepper & cook for 5 minutes. Add chopped tofu & cook for 5 minutes. Serve topped with chopped salted peanuts, lime juice, & chopped cilantro.

18. Shrimp Lo Mein

Shrimp and noodles!

Serving: 2
Preparation Time: 20 minutes

Ingredients

- Chinese noodles/ Spaghetti (8 oz.)
- Water (1 tbsp.)
- Shrimp (8 oz., peeled and deveined)
- Cornstarch (1 teaspoon)
- Oil (4 tablespoons)
- Garlic (3 cloves, minced)
- Napa Cabbage (1 cup, sliced)
- Shiitake Mushroom (2, sliced)
- Carrots (1/3 cup, chopped)
- Shrimp broth (1/2 cup)
- Sauce
- Soy sauce (1 tablespoon)
- Oyster Sauce (1 teaspoon)
- Sesame Oil (1/4 teaspoon)

- White Pepper (1/4 tsp)
- Sugar (1/4 tsp)
- Salt (1/4 tsp)

Method

1. Boil noodles as directed on package, drain and put aside till needed. Mix cornstarch with shrimp and set aside.
2. Heat oil in a wok and brown garlic then add shrimp, mushroom, cabbage, carrot and cook for 2 minutes.
3. Add your sauce ingredients and broth then lower heat; reduce liquid and take away from the flame. Add noodles, toss and serve hot.

19. Salmon & Snow Pea Stir Fry

A delicious & fresh fish dish that is a great way to pack in Omega fatty acids

Serves: 2
Time to Prepare: 15 min

Ingredients

- 6 oz Chopped Skinless Salmon Fillet
- 1/4 cup Soy Sauce
- 1/4 cup Orange Juice
- 1 Minced Garlic Clove
- 1 Tsp Sesame Oil
- 1 Tbsp Peanut Oil
- 1 Sliced Onion
- 6 oz Snow Peas

Method

1. In a bowl, mix soy sauce, orange juice, minced garlic, & sesame oil. Set aside 1/2 of the sauce & place chopped salmon in bowl. Marinade for 30 minutes. Discard marinade.
2. In a wok or large frying pan, add oil & salmon. Cook for 5 minutes. Remove & set aside.
3. Add sliced onion & sauté for 5 minutes. Add snow peas & cook for 3 minutes. Add salmon & reserved marinade. Cook for 3 minutes & serve.

20. Bacon Fried Rice

A super simple dinner that still pleases with sweet & smoky flavors

Serves: 4
Time to Prepare: 5 min

Ingredients

- 4 cups Cold Cooked Rice
- 2 Chopped Slices Bacon
- 6 Sliced Green Onions
- 1 Beaten Egg
- Soy Sauce (2 Tbsp)
- 1/2 Tsp Garlic Powder

Method

1. Cook bacon until crispy. This can be done in a frying pan or in the oven. In a wok or large frying pan, add oil, bacon, & sliced green onion. Sauté for 1 minute.

2. Add egg & cook for 2 minutes. Add rice & garlic powder. Fry for 5-10 minutes. Add soy sauce & serve.

Chicken stir fry recipes

Stir fry chicken and vegetables

Description: This chicken stir fry recipe is very easy and simple to make with only a few ingredients and can be served with rice.

Preparation time: 40 minutes
Servings: 2

Ingredients:

- Boneless chicken- 6 ounces
- Soya sauce- 2 tablespoons
- Sherry- 2 tablespoons
- Cornstarch- 1 tablespoon
- Oil- 1 tablespoon

- Broccoli florets- 1 cup
- Green pepper- 1
- Zucchini- 1 cup
- Garlic cloves- 3
- Chicken broth- ½ cup
- Oil- 1 tablespoon
- Green onions- 6

Recipe:

- Mix the chicken, soya sauce, sherry and cornstarch in a bowl.
- Heat oil in a wok and fry the broccoli florets, bell pepper, zucchini and the garlic cloves for a few minutes.
- Add the chicken broth, cover and let cook for a few minutes.
- Empty and clean the pan in a bowl.
- Heat oil in the pan and add the chicken mixture and fry until the chicken is cooked.
- Stir in the vegetables and chop green onions and garnish.
- Serve with rice.

Kung pao chicken

Description: This is a spicy stir fry chicken recipe with peanuts. It is like a Chinese dish and can be served with rice.

Preparation time: 1 hour
Servings: 4

Ingredients:

- Boneless chicken- 1 pound
- White wine- 2 tablespoons
- Soya sauce- 2 tablespoon
- Sesame oil- 2 tablespoon
- Cornstarch- 2 tablespoon
- Chili paste- 1 ounce
- Vinegar- 1 teaspoon
- Brown sugar- 2 teaspoon
- Green onions- 4

- Garlic clove- 1
- Water chestnuts- 1 can
- Chopped peanuts- 4 ounce

Recipe:

- Marinate the chicken with half of the white wine, soya sauce, oil and cornstarch.
- For the sauce, mix the remaining wine, soya sauce, oil, cornstarch, chili paste, vinegar and sugar.
- Mix and now add the green onion, garlic, water chestnuts and the peanuts.
- Heat the sauce in a pan.
- Add the chicken in the sauce and simmer until sauce thickens.
- Serve with rice!

Sweet and spicy stir fry chicken with broccoli

Description: This sweet and spicy stir fry chicken is very tasty because of the ginger, chili paste and hoisin sauce. This is served with jasmine rice.

Preparation time: 30 minutes
Servings: 4

Ingredients:

- Broccoli florets- 3 cup
- Olive oil- 1 tablespoon
- Boneless chicken breast- 2
- Green onions- ¼ cup
- Garlic cloves- 4
- Hoisin sauce- 1 tablespoon
- Chile paste- 1 tablespoon
- Soya sauce- 1 tablespoon
- Ginger- ½ teaspoon

- Red pepper- ¼ teaspoon
- Salt- ½ teaspoon
- Black pepper- ½ teaspoon
- Chicken stock- 1/8 cup

Recipe:

- Steam the broccoli florets until tender.
- Heat oil in a pan and fry the green onions, chicken, and the garlic until chicken is cooked.
- Add the hoisin sauce, chile paste and the soya sauce.
- Now add the red pepper, ginger, salt and black pepper to taste.
- Now add the chicken stock, cover and let cook.
- Finally add the broccoli florets.
- Serve!

Cashew chicken stir fry with cauliflower rice

Description: This chicken stir fry dish is low in carbs and healthy as well. It is made with just a few ingredients.

Preparation time: 15 minutes
Servings: 4

Ingredients:

- Cauliflower- 1 head
- Olive oil- 1 tablespoon
- Salt- a pinch
- Chili sauce- ¼ cup
- Soya sauce- 3 tablespoon
- Sriracha sauce- 1 tablespoon
- Garlic clove- 1
- Lemon juice- 1
- Sesame oil- 1 tablespoon

- Red pepper- 2
- Zucchini- 1
- Boneless chicken breast- 2
- Cashews- ½ cup

Recipe:

- Pulse the cauliflower heads in a blender until they form the consistency of rice.
- In a pan, add oil and the cauliflower rice and add salt.
- In another bowl, make the sauce by mixing the chili sauce, soya sauce, Sriracha sauce, lemon juice and the garlic.
- In another pan, heat the sesame oil and fry the red pepper and the zucchini for few minutes.
- Add the chicken and the sauce.
- Now add the cashews and let the chicken cook.
- Serve with cauliflower rice.

Simple chicken teriyaki stir fry

Description: This chicken teriyaki stir fry is the most favorite Chinese dish loved by people all over the world. Its sauce and juicy chicken is what makes it most appealing.

Preparation time: 30 minutes

Servings: 5

Ingredients:

- Onion- 1
- Broccoli heads- 2
- Green capsicum- 1
- Sesame oil- 1 tablespoon
- Chicken boneless cubes- 500 grams
- Soya sauce- ¼ cup
- Rice wine- ¼ cup
- Brown sugar- ¼ cup
- Sake- 2 tablespoon

- Garlic- 1 teaspoon
- Green onion- a handful

Recipe:

- Steam the onion, broccoli heads and the capsicum.
- In a pan, heat the sesame oil and stir fry the chicken.
- In another pan, make the sauce by adding soya sauce, mirin, sake, brown sugar and the garlic and cook.
- Add the chicken and steamed vegetables in the sauce and mix.
- Garnish with green onions and serve!

Chicken, kale and sprout stir fry

Description: Sprouts are not only served during Christmas. You can add health and nutrition to your everyday chicken meal.

Preparation time: 10 minutes
Servings: 2

Ingredients:

- Soba noodle- 100 grams
- Kale- 100 grams
- Sesame oil- 2 teaspoon
- Chicken breast- 2
- Ginger- 1 tablespoon
- Red pepper- 1
- Brussel sprouts- 1 bunch
- Soya sauce- 1 tablespoon
- Rice wine- 2 tablespoon
- Lemon juice- 1

Recipe:

- Cook the soba noodles.
- Heat 1 tablespoon of sesame oil and stir fry the chicken.
- Heat the remaining sesame oil in another pan and fry the ginger, pepper and the sprouts.
- Add in the chicken, noodles and the kale.
- Now add in the soya sauce, rice wine and the lemon juice and mix.
- Serve!

General Tso's chicken stir fry

Description: This is an exceptionally delicious recipe of a stir fry chicken with a yummy sauce.

Preparation time: 40 minutes

Servings: 4

Ingredients:

- Boneless chicken- 4
- Cornstarch- ½ cup + 2 tablespoon
- Flour- 1 cup
- Oil- 1 tablespoon
- Black pepper- a pinch
- Red pepper flakes- 1 teaspoon

- Garlic cloves- 2
- Chicken broth- ½ cup
- Hoisin sauce- 2 tablespoon
- Honey- 3 tablespoon
- Soya sauce- 4 tablespoon
- Lemon juice- 2 tablespoon
- Broccoli florets- 1 head
- Carrots- 2
- Sesame seeds for garnishing

Recipe:

- In a bowl, marinate the chicken cubes with half cup of cornstarch and flour.
- In a pan, heat the oil and fry the chicken until it is cooked.
- Sprinkle pepper.
- Now add the garlic clove and the red pepper.
- Add the chicken broth, hoisin sauce, soya sauce, honey and lemon juice.
- Add the rest of the cornstarch and let cook.
- Add the broccoli florets and the sliced carrots and mix everything.
- Serve!

10 minutes stir fry chicken recipe

Description: This is the perfect stir fry chicken recipe for those who want to have a quick lunch and wish to eat low carbs.

Preparation time: 5 minutes

Servings: 4

Ingredients:

- Vegetable oil- 1 tablespoon
- Red chili- 1
- Garlic clove- 1
- Mix vegetables- 500 grams
- Soya sauce- 1.5 tablespoon
- Sweet chili sauce- 2 tablespoon
- Shredded chicken- 1 cup

Recipe:

- Heat oil in a wok and fry the garlic and the red chili.
- Add the mix vegetables and the shredded chicken and fry until the chicken is cooked.
- Now add the soya sauce and chili sauce.
- Cook until the vegetables are tender and the chicken is cooked.
- Serve!

Addictive Sesame Chicken

Serving: 4 | Prep: 30mins | Cook: 20mins | Ready in:
Ingredients

2 tablespoons soy sauce

1 tablespoon dry sherry

1 dash sesame oil

2 tablespoons all-purpose flour

2 tablespoons cornstarch

2 tablespoons water

1/4 teaspoon baking powder

1/4 teaspoon baking soda

1 teaspoon canola oil

4 (5 ounce) skinless, boneless chicken breast halves, cut into 1-inch cubes

1 quart vegetable oil for frying

1/2 cup water

1 cup chicken broth

1/4 cup distilled white vinegar

1/4 cup cornstarch

1 cup white sugar

2 tablespoons soy sauce

2 tablespoons sesame oil

1 teaspoon red chile paste (such as Thai Kitchen®)

1 clove garlic, minced

2 tablespoons toasted sesame seeds

Direction

Mix canola oil, baking soda, baking powder, 2 tbsp. water, 2 tbsp. cornstarch, flour, dash of sesame oil, dry sherry and 2 tbsp. soy sauce well in big bowl; mix chicken in. Cover; refrigerate for 20 minutes.

Heat oil to 190°C/375°F in big saucepan/deep fryer.

Mix garlic, red chili paste, 2 tbsp. sesame oil, 2 tbsp. soy sauce, sugar, 1/4 cup cornstarch, vinegar, chicken broth and 1/2 cup water in small saucepan, let the mixture come to a boil; constantly mix. Turn heat to low; keep warm, occasionally mixing.

Fry marinated chicken for 3-5 minutes in batches till golden brown and cooked through; drain on paper towels.

Put chicken on big platter; put sauce over. Sprinkle sesame seeds on top.

Nutrition Information

Calories: 745 calories;

Cholesterol: 88

Protein: 34.3

Total Fat: 37.1

Sodium: 1405

Total Carbohydrate: 68.6

Adriel's Chinese Curry Chicken

Serving: 4 | Prep: 25mins | Cook: 25mins | Ready in:
Ingredients

1 tablespoon yellow curry paste

1/2 cup chicken broth, divided

1 teaspoon white sugar

1 1/2 teaspoons curry powder

1/2 teaspoon salt

4 1/2 teaspoons light soy sauce

1 (5.6 ounce) can coconut milk

1 tablespoon canola oil

3 skinless, boneless chicken breast halves, sliced

2 teaspoons minced garlic

1 teaspoon minced fresh ginger

1 onion, sliced

2 potatoes - peeled, halved, and sliced

Direction

Smash yellow curry paste in a large bowl together with 2 tbsp. of chicken broth to dissolve the paste. Stir in the remaining chicken broth, light soy sauce, salt, coconut milk, sugar, and curry powder into the bowl. Set aside.

Warm skillet over high heat for 30 seconds. Add oil and allow it to heat until glistening, approximately half a minute. Cook and stir ginger, garlic, and chicken for about 2 minutes until garlic and ginger are fragrant and the chicken starts to brown. Add potatoes and onion and toss to combine. Pour in the sauce mixture and let it boil. Lower the heat and cover the skillet. Let it simmer for 20-25 minutes until the potatoes are tender and the chicken is completely cooked.

Nutrition Information

Calories: 241 calories;

Cholesterol: 46

Protein: 20.1

Total Fat: 7.1

Sodium: 864

Total Carbohydrate: 24.1

Almond Vegetable Chicken Stir Fry

Serving: 5 servings. | Prep: 5mins | Cook: 10mins | Ready in:

Ingredients

1 pound boneless skinless chicken breasts, cut into thin strips
3/4 cup sliced almonds
1 tablespoon canola oil
1 package (16 ounces) frozen broccoli stir-fry vegetable blend
1 tablespoon cornstarch
1 tablespoon brown sugar
1/2 teaspoon ground ginger
1/3 cup unsweetened pineapple juice
1/3 cup reduced-sodium soy sauce
Hot cooked rice, optional

Direction

Stir-fry the almonds and chicken in a wok or large nonstick skillet with oil for 2 minutes. Add the vegetables. Adjust the heat to low. Cover the skillet and cook for 4 minutes until the chicken is not anymore pinkish and the vegetables turn tender.

Mix the brown sugar, ginger, and cornstarch in a small bowl. Mix in soy sauce and pineapple juice until smooth. Mix the mixture into the chicken mixture; boil. Cook for 2 minutes, stirring until thickened. If desired, serve this with rice.

Nutrition Information

Calories: 278 calories

Cholesterol: 54mg cholesterol

Protein: 26g protein. Diabetic Exchanges: 3 lean meat

Total Fat: 11g fat (1g saturated fat)

Sodium: 708mg sodium

Fiber: 3g fiber)

Total Carbohydrate: 17g carbohydrate (0 sugars

Anise Wine Chicken

Serving: 4 | Prep: 30mins | Cook: 25mins | Ready in:
Ingredients

1 small onion, chopped

2 inch piece fresh ginger root, minced

2 cloves garlic, minced

2 whole star anise pods

1/2 cup dry white wine

1 teaspoon salt

1/4 teaspoon ground black pepper

2 tablespoons vegetable oil

1 teaspoon rice vinegar

1/2 pound skinless, boneless chicken breast meat - cut into bite-size pieces

20 new potatoes

1 tablespoon vegetable oil

1 cup cherry tomatoes

1 tablespoon cornstarch

2 tablespoons water

1/4 cup minced fresh Thai basil leaves

Direction

Combine chicken, 2 tbsp. of vegetable oil, star anise, salt, onion, white wine, rice vinegar, garlic, pepper, and ginger together in a large mixing bowl. Cover the bowl and place it inside the refrigerator to marinate for 4-6 hours. While waiting, cover potatoes with salted water inside a large pot. Let it boil over high heat. Adjust the heat to medium-low and cover the pot to simmer for 15 minutes until the potatoes are tender. Drain the potatoes and cool before cutting them into halves.

Spread 1 tbsp. of vegetable oil into a large skillet and heat it over high heat. Take the chicken out of the marinade, squeezing off any excess, and cook it into the heated oil for 5 minutes until the center is no longer pink in the middle and the sides are all browned. Reserve the marinade for the next step. Discard star anise from the reserved marinade. Pour the marinade all over the chicken and bring it to boil. Stir in halved potatoes and cherry tomatoes and cook for 3 minutes until the potatoes are hot and the cherry tomatoes start to burst. Dissolve cornstarch in the water and add it into the chicken mixture together with Thai basil. Cook for 1 more minute, stirring it frequently until thick.

Nutrition Information

Calories: 562 calories;

Total Carbohydrate: 87.8

Cholesterol: 33

Protein: 23.3

Total Fat: 11.6

Sodium: 653

Apricot Chicken Stir Fry

Serving: 4 servings. | Prep: 10mins | Cook: 20mins | Ready in:

Ingredients

1/2 cup dried apricot halves, cut in half

1/4 cup hot water

1 tablespoon all-purpose flour

1 tablespoon chopped cilantro, optional

1/2 teaspoon salt

1/8 teaspoon pepper

3/4 pound boneless skinless chicken breasts, cut into 1/2-inch pieces

3 tablespoons canola oil, divided

1 medium onion, halved and sliced

1 cup chopped celery

1/2 cup halved snow peas

1/2 teaspoon ground ginger

1 garlic clove, minced

1 to 2 tablespoons lemon juice

Hot cooked rice

Direction

Steep apricots in a small bowl of water; put to one side (do not drain). Combine pepper, salt, flour, and cilantro (if desired); scatter over the chicken and put to one side.

In a wok or large skillet, heat 1 tablespoon oil over medium heat; sauté celery and onion in heated oil until tender, about 2 to 3 minutes. Add apricots, garlic, ginger, and peas; sauté for 2 minutes. Take everything out and keep warm.

Add the rest of oil to the skillet; cook and stir chicken until no longer pink, about 6 to 7 minutes. Add lemon juice to the skillet. Pour apricot mixture back into the skillet and cook until heated through. Serve warm with rice.

Nutrition Information

Calories: 268 calories

Sodium: 364mg sodium

Fiber: 4g fiber)

Total Carbohydrate: 20g carbohydrate (12g sugars

Cholesterol: 47mg cholesterol

Protein: 19g protein.

Total Fat: 12g fat (2g saturated fat)

Apricot Chicken And Snow Peas

Serving: 1 serving. | Prep: 5mins | Cook: 15mins | Ready in:

Ingredients

1/4 pound boneless skinless chicken breasts, cut into thin strips

1/2 teaspoon canola oil

1/2 cup fresh snow peas

3 tablespoons apricot preserves

2 tablespoons water

1 small garlic clove, minced

3/4 teaspoon sesame oil

1/2 teaspoon sesame seeds, toasted

1/2 teaspoon soy sauce

1/8 teaspoon Dijon mustard

1/8 teaspoon ground ginger

Hot cooked rice

Direction

Stir-fry chicken in oil in a big wok or skillet, about 3 minutes. Add ginger, mustard, soy sauce, sesame seeds, sesame oil, garlic, water, preserves, and snow peas. Boil. Lower the heat and simmer without a cover until the vegetables are soft and chicken juices run clear, about 5-7 minutes. Enjoy with rice.

Nutrition Information

Calories: 365 calories

Sodium: 258mg sodium

Fiber: 3g fiber)

Total Carbohydrate: 46g carbohydrate (25g sugars

Cholesterol: 63mg cholesterol

Protein: 26g protein.

Total Fat: 9g fat (2g saturated fat)

Asian Breakfast Stir Fry

Serving: 1 | Prep: 20mins | Cook: 35mins | Ready in:

Ingredients

1 cup water

1/2 cup quinoa

1 large carrot, peeled and chopped

1/2 cup broccoli florets

1/4 cup chopped onion

1 (1 inch) piece ginger, peeled, or to taste

1 tablespoon sesame oil

1 tablespoon minced garlic

1 cup kale

1 tablespoon reduced-sodium soy sauce

1 tablespoon water

1/2 cup shredded boneless, skinless baked chicken breast

1 cooking spray (optional)

2 large eggs

1 teaspoon chile-garlic sauce (such as Sriracha®), or to taste (optional)

1 teaspoon fresh cilantro, or to taste (optional)

1 teaspoon sesame seeds, or to taste (optional)

Direction

In a saucepan, bring water and quinoa to a boil. Lower heat to medium-low, cover, and simmer for 15-20 mins, until the quinoa is tender.

In the bowl of a food processor, combine onion, carrot and broccoli and chop.

In a large skillet, heat sesame oil over medium heat and put in garlic. Whisk for a minute, until fragrant. Put in chopped vegetable mixture from the food processor. Cook and stir for 3 to 5 mins or until the onions are translucent. Put in kale. Cook for a minute or until wilted. Pour water and soy sauce over the mixture. Cook 5 more mins.

Add 1/4 cup of cooked quinoa and chicken to the skillet with vegetable mixture. Cook and stir for 2-3 mins or until heated through. Place stir-fry to the plate.

Coat the skillet with cooking spray. Cook eggs 3-5 mins to preference. In the plate, put cooked eggs on the top of stir-fry. Garnish with sesame seeds, cilantro and chile-garlic sauce.

Nutrition Information

Calories: 814 calories;
Sodium: 1015
Total Carbohydrate: 75.4
Cholesterol: 424
Protein: 48.2
Total Fat: 36.1

Asian Carryout Noodles

Serving: 2 | Prep: 20mins | Cook: 30mins | Ready in:

Ingredients

1 (8 ounce) package angel hair pasta
1 teaspoon canola oil
1 teaspoon sesame oil
1/2 onion, chopped
1 clove garlic, minced
1 skinless, boneless chicken breast half - cut into bite-size pieces
1 tablespoon grated fresh ginger
2 leaves bok choy, diced
1/4 cup chicken broth
2 tablespoons dry sherry
1 tablespoon soy sauce
1 1/2 tablespoons hoisin sauce
1/8 teaspoon salt
2 green onions, minced

Direction

Boil a large pot of salted water and cook the angel hair pasta until it becomes al dente, then drain.

At the same time, heat sesame and canola oil in a big nonstick skillet on medium high heat, then sauté garlic and onions until soft. Stir in the chopped chicken and cook until brown and its juices are clear. Stir in hoisin sauce, soy sauce, sherry, chicken stock, bok choy, and ginger. Lower the heat and continue to cook for 10 minutes.

Toss in the pasta with the chicken mixture until coated and season with salt. Serve warm with a sprinkling of minced green onion.

Nutrition Information

Calories: 499 calories;

Sodium: 1257

Total Carbohydrate: 75.4

Cholesterol: 35

Protein: 28.1

Total Fat: 9.2

Asian Chicken With Pasta

Serving: 6 servings. | Prep: 15mins | Cook: 10mins | Ready in:

Ingredients
1/2 pound uncooked angel hair pasta
1 pound chicken tenderloins, cut into 1-inch cubes
1/3 cup prepared balsamic vinaigrette
1/3 cup prepared Italian salad dressing
1 package (12 ounces) broccoli coleslaw mix
1/2 pound sliced fresh mushrooms
3/4 cup julienned sweet red pepper
1/2 cup sliced onion
1/2 teaspoon garlic powder

1/2 teaspoon ground ginger
1/4 teaspoon salt
1/8 teaspoon pepper

Direction

Follow the package cooking instructions to cook pasta. At the same time, sauté chicken in salad dressing and vinaigrette in a big skillet until not pink anymore. Remove and keep warm.

Sauté onion, red pepper, mushrooms, coleslaw mix in the same skillet until soft. Put in seasonings. Mix in chicken; heat through. Strain pasta. Put into the chicken mixture; toss to coat.

Nutrition Information

Calories: 320 calories
Protein: 25g protein. Diabetic Exchanges: 3 lean meat
Total Fat: 8g fat (1g saturated fat)
Sodium: 474mg sodium
Fiber: 4g fiber)
Total Carbohydrate: 38g carbohydrate (6g sugars
Cholesterol: 44mg cholesterol

Asian Chicken With Peanuts

Serving: 4 | Prep: 15mins | Cook: 20mins | Ready in:

Ingredients

2 tablespoons cornstarch

1 3/4 cups Swanson® Chicken Stock

2 tablespoons soy sauce

1/2 teaspoon ground ginger

1/2 teaspoon sesame oil (optional)

2 tablespoons vegetable oil

1 pound skinless, boneless chicken breast, cut into strips

2 cups broccoli florets

2 small red peppers, cut into 2-inch-long strips

2 cloves garlic, minced

1/2 cup salted peanuts

4 cups Hot cooked regular long-grain white rice

Direction

In a medium mixing bowl, combine ginger, soy sauce, stock, cornstarch, and sesame oil (if using) until no lumps remain.

Heat 1 tablespoon vegetable oil over medium-high heat in a 12-inch skillet. Sauté chicken in the heated oil until all sides are browned; stir frequently. Take chicken out of the skillet.

Lower heat to medium. Heat the rest of the vegetable oil in the skillet. Sauté garlic, peppers, and broccoli in hot oil until vegetables are tender but crisp. Whisk cornstarch mixture into the skillet. Cook, stirring, until mixture is boiling and thickened. Put chicken back into the skillet. Mix in peanuts; keep cooking until mixture is bubbly and heated through. Spoon over rice to serve.

Nutrition Information

Calories: 561 calories;

Cholesterol: 65

Protein: 36.2

Total Fat: 19.9

Sodium: 898

Total Carbohydrate: 59.1

Authentic Thai Basil Chicken (Very Easy And Fast)

Serving: 2 | Prep: 15mins | Cook: 9mins | Ready in:
Ingredients

2 tablespoons vegetable oil

1/2 onion, sliced

3 cloves garlic, sliced

1 large skinless, boneless chicken breast, cut into 1-inch pieces

1/4 cup oyster sauce

3 tablespoons soy sauce

1 pinch white sugar

2 small chile peppers, sliced (optional)

1/3 cup water

1/2 cup fresh basil leaves

Direction

Heat oil over medium heat in a large skillet or wok. Sauté garlic and onion in heated oil for about half a minute until aromatic. Stir in chicken; sauté for about 5 minutes until no longer pink inside. Mix in sugar, soy sauce, and oyster sauce. Add chile peppers; stir to combine. Add water into the skillet. Cook for 3 to 5 minutes until mixture thickens slightly. Mix in basil just before serving.

Nutrition Information

Calories: 304 calories;

Protein: 25.8

Total Fat: 16.2

Sodium: 1625

Total Carbohydrate: 14.5

Cholesterol: 59

Avocado Chicken Stir Fry

Serving: 4 | Prep: 25mins | Cook: 15mins | Ready in:
Ingredients

1/2 cup chicken broth

1/4 cup soy sauce

1 tablespoon cornstarch

1 clove garlic, minced

1 tablespoon vegetable oil

4 skinless, boneless chicken breast halves, cut into bite size pieces

2 cups snow peas

2 cups cremini mushrooms, stems discarded, caps thinly sliced

4 bunches green onions, cut into 1-inch pieces

2 large ripe but firm avocados - peeled, pitted, and cut into large chunks

Direction

Mix garlic, cornstarch, soy sauce, and chicken broth in a bowl until cornstarch turns smooth, set aside.

Place a large skillet or wok on the stove and turn on to medium-high heat. Put oil until sparkling. Stir and cook the chicken for about 5 minutes until meat is no longer pink in the middle and is cooked through. Remove from skillet or wok and set aside. Put snow peas into hot wok or skillet. Stir and cook for about 3 minutes until bright green in color yet still crisp. Mix in the green onions and mushrooms, and cook for about 5 minutes until mushrooms are softened and have given up their juice. Get rid of extra juices, if there is.

Put the chicken back to wok. Mix briefly over medium heat to combine with the cooked vegetables. Pour the reserved sauce ingredients to remix, if necessary, and place to the wok. Slowly mix in the avocado, and allow the mixture to bubble for about 3 minutes until the sauce turns thick. Mix slowly to cover everything in sauce, then serve.

Nutrition Information

Calories: 494 calories;

Total Carbohydrate: 36.8

Cholesterol: 61

Protein: 33.4

Total Fat: 27.3

Sodium: 1002

Basil Chicken Medley

Serving: 4 servings. | Prep: 10mins | Cook: 15mins | Ready in:

Ingredients

1 tablespoon olive oil

3 garlic cloves, minced

2 whole boneless, skinless chicken breasts (about 1-1/4 pounds), cut into 1-inch chunks

1 medium zucchini, cut into chunks

2 medium tomatoes, cut into chunks

1 tablespoon dried basil

2 tablespoons vinegar

1/4 teaspoon pepper

Cooked rice or pasta

Direction

In skillet, heat the oil; sauté the garlic. Put in and cook chicken till not anymore pink; take and retain warmth. Mix pepper, vinegar, basil, tomato and zucchini, toss till vegetables are coated thoroughly.

Put into skillet and stir-fry, for 3 minutes to 5 minutes. Put chicken back to skillet and heat completely. Serve right away on top of pasta or rice.

Nutrition Information

Calories: 205 calories

Cholesterol: 73mg cholesterol

Protein: 28g protein. Diabetic Exchanges: 3 lean meat

Total Fat: 7g fat (0 saturated fat)

Sodium: 70mg sodium

Fiber: 0 fiber)

Total Carbohydrate: 8g carbohydrate (0 sugars

Bow Tie Chicken Supper

Serving: 4 servings. | Prep: 15mins | Cook: 15mins | Ready in:

Ingredients

1 pound boneless skinless chicken breasts, cut into 1/4-inch strips

1 tablespoon olive oil

1 small sweet red pepper, julienned

1 small zucchini, cut into 1/4-inch slices

1 small onion, chopped

2 garlic cloves, minced

1/2 cup frozen peas, thawed

1 teaspoon Italian seasoning

1/4 teaspoon salt-free seasoning blend

1 cup bow tie pasta, cooked and drained

2 medium tomatoes, seeded and chopped

1/4 cup shredded Parmesan cheese

Direction

In a large nonstick frying pan, sauté chicken in oil until no longer pink or 3 to 5 mins. Discard and keep warm. Stir-fry garlic, onion, zucchini and red pepper in the same skillet, until the vegetables are crisp-tender or 3 to 4 mins.

Put in seasonings and peas; stir-fry for 2 mins. Put in tomatoes and pasta; cook for a minute. Take away from heat. Gently stir in the chicken. Top with a sprinkle of cheese.

Nutrition Information

Calories: 256 calories

Sodium: 219mg sodium

Fiber: 3g fiber)

Total Carbohydrate: 15g carbohydrate (0 sugars

Cholesterol: 71mg cholesterol

Protein: 32g protein. Diabetic Exchanges: 3 lean meat

Total Fat: 7g fat (2g saturated fat)

Broccoli Chicken Stir Fry

Serving: 4 servings. | Prep: 5mins | Cook: 25mins | Ready in:

Ingredients

1 pound boneless skinless chicken breasts, cut into 1-inch pieces

1 tablespoon canola oil

2 cups fresh broccoli florets

1 small sweet red pepper, julienned

1 can (8 ounces) sliced water chestnuts, drained

1 package (6 ounces) frozen snow peas, thawed

1 small onion, cut into thin wedges

2 garlic cloves, minced

1 teaspoon Chinese Five Spice

1 can (14-1/2 ounces) chicken broth

2 tablespoons cornstarch

2 tablespoons cold water

4 cups hot cooked rice

Direction

Stir-fry chicken in oil in a wok or large nonstick skillet until slightly browned and juices run clear, about 8 minutes. Remove from the pan and keep warm. Sauté garlic, onion, snow peas, water chestnuts, red pepper, and broccoli in the same skillet for 6 to 8 minutes until crisp-tender.

Add chicken back to the pan; scatter with Chinese five spice. Mix in broth; bring to a boil. Whisk together cold water and cornstarch until no lumps remain; slowly stir into the skillet. Cook, stirring, until thickened, about 2 minutes. Serve over rice.

Nutrition Information

Calories: 459 calories

Sodium: 504mg sodium

Fiber: 6g fiber)

Total Carbohydrate: 65g carbohydrate (0 sugars

Cholesterol: 66mg cholesterol

Protein: 35g protein.

Total Fat: 6g fat (1g saturated fat)

Broccoli Chicken Stir Fry For Two

Serving: 2 servings. | Prep: 15mins | Cook: 15mins | Ready in:

Ingredients

1/2 medium spaghetti squash
SAUCE:
1/2 cup chicken broth
4-1/2 teaspoons soy sauce
1 tablespoon sugar
1 tablespoon cornstarch
1 tablespoon cider vinegar
Dash crushed red pepper flakes
STIR-FRY:
2 tablespoons beaten egg
1-1/2 teaspoons soy sauce
1/4 cup cornstarch
1/2 pound boneless skinless chicken breasts, cut into 1-inch cubes
2 tablespoons canola oil
1 cup fresh broccoli florets
1/4 cup chopped onion

Direction

Put squash in microwave-safe dish, cut side down. Microwave for 10-12 minutes till tender on high, uncovered.

Meanwhile, mix pepper flakes, vinegar, cornstarch, sugar, soy sauce and broth till smooth in small bowl; put aside.

Whisk soy sauce and egg in shallow bowl. Put cornstarch in separate shallow bowl. In egg mixture, dip chicken; coat with cornstarch. In batches, stir-fry chicken in oil in big skillet/wok till not pink; remove. Keep warm.

Stir-fry onion and broccoli till crisp-tender for 2-3 minutes. Mix cornstarch mixture; add into pan. Boil; mix and cook till thick for 1-2 minutes. Add chicken and heat through.

Use fork to separate strands when squash is cool to handle. Serve with stir-fry.

Nutrition Information

Calories: 501 calories

Total Carbohydrate: 51g carbohydrate (8g sugars

Cholesterol: 128mg cholesterol

Protein: 30g protein.

Total Fat: 20g fat (3g saturated fat)

Sodium: 1308mg sodium

Fiber: 6g fiber)

www.ingramcontent.com/pod-product-compliance
Lightning Source LLC
Chambersburg PA
CBHW071438070526
44578CB00001B/136